STRANGE
POEMS

STRANGE POEMS

From the Garden to Heaven
XX and XXl Centuries

By Lorenzo Amado Periú

ISBN: 978-1-965679-63-0 (sc)
ISBN: 978-1-965679-64-7 (e)

Rev. date: 12/11/2024

CONTENTS

"VARIABILITY/DIVERGENT"

DIFFERENCES OF TRUTHS,
DIVERSE, UNIVERSAL,
UNIQUE,
DYNAMIC, DIVINE
LIKE NATURE;
OF MILLIONS OF
DIFFERENT SPECIES.
WE LIVE IN THIS WORLD.
AND STILL IN
THE 21ST CENTURY,
WITH COMPUTERS
HIGH TECHNOLOGY,
AND CELL PHONES
THAT DO
ALMOST EVERYTHING
LESS A LOT OF FUN THINGS,
NOT CALCULATED,
NOR PRESUMED,
WHERE
THE SCIENTIFIC ADVANCE,
THERMO NUCLEAR AND
TECHNOLOGICAL
HAS REACHED IRREFLEXIBLES
GREAT MODERN ADVANCES
TO IMPROVE
HUMAN CONDITIONS
OF ALL GOD'S CREATURES.
SO THAT IT LASTS
AND PROSPERS ALWAYS
THE SO-CALLED PLANET EARTH;
SACRED KINGDOM IN THE SPACES

INFINITES OF HEAVEN.
WE ARE ALREADY IN
THE AGE OF AQUARIUS
AND
THE DRAMATIC SITUATIONS
THEY CONTINUE TO HAPPEN
AS
THEY HAVE ALWAYS HAPPENED,
FROM THE VERY BEGINNING
OF ORIGINAL SIN;
THE SAME THINGS
KEEP BEING REPEATED TODAY
AND THEY ARE GETTING WORSE
AND WORSE.
EXPELLING TRAGEDIES
AND DRAMAS;
SINCE DANTE'S
AND BEFORE HE WROTE;
THE DIVINE COMEDY,
WE ALREADY LIVE IT,
AND WE HAVE TO KEEP
LIVING LIKE THIS
OUR INDISCUTABLE TRUTH,
IN THE DESPERATE ADVANCE...
OF DAILY SURVIVAL FOREVER
TO CONTINUE BEING
THE CLASSICS OF THE FUTURE
EACH ONE IN
THEIR ORIGINAL PAPER...
IN ITS MARKED
TIME OF DESTINY
FOR THE INVISIBLE HOUR
OF SUSPENSE,
THAT NO ONE

WILL KNOW HIS LAST BREATH
WHERE WILL IT BE.
REPRODUCTION,
TRANSFORMATION, PAIN.
AMAZING DISCOVERIES
WILL COME
AND EVEN THOUGH
WE KNOW THAT
EVERYTHING IS TO DIE;
BY THE BIOLOGICAL
CYCLE OF LIFE;
WE HAVE OUR TIME TO LIVE,
WITH THE SAME
ESSENCE OF THE UNIVERSE
WHO CREATED US WISELY
LIKE MORTAL BEINGS
IN THIS RISKY WORLD
THAT ONE DAY
WILL DISAPPEAR.

*

"YOU'RE LAUGHTER"

You laugh so sweetly...
That leaves me ecstatic.
And I feel...
More in love
When I see you laugh.
Your laugh is like living
In a world of illusions.
Your laughter calms
my fears,
And it makes me smile.
Laugh at me if you want.
Laugh, with more candor,
That soon I will
bite the flower,
what form your
beautiful lips...
And you won't feel
any grievance
When I possesses you;
Because you will
laugh happier
When I kiss your mouth...
And turn off your crazy laugh,
Overshadowing the crimson.

*

"AFTER"

After I looked
for you
to love you;
What else can I say?
After we talked
the first night,
When you come back here.
Life grabbed me again,
To live it for you.
It was what
I wanted most...
When I didn't
have you;
I ceased to
belong to me.
My soul had
given you before
All the love I felt.
When I accidentally
met you.
Without receiving
anything in return;
Of this passion
so strong
That sentimentally
makes me happy.
Even if I live only
to love you...
Without kissing you,
or hugging you...
Even if I only live...

To love you...
In this house,
Not expecting
anything yet.
I like life more,
Because
I'm full of love
For you every day.
I prefer to live
like this,
it's less sad,
I already tasted
my loneliness
when you left,
And
in that adversity
I didn't stop
missing you
Every second of
the day.
Tonight under
the Virgo;s moon
we are together
Living again
under
the same roof
In separate
beds sleeping...
With you here,
I can control
my life better...
Although
the control of
your helm

for our ship
Of white sails...
Continue drifting.

August 6, 1987

"DEATH"

SHE LOOKED AT ME,
BUT I DIDN'T SEE HER;
DEATH WAS THERE;
SHE CALLED ME,
AND I DIDN'T
ANSWER HER;
DEATH WAS THERE;
SHE WHISTLED AT ME
AND I DIDN'T GO;
DEATH WAS THERE;
I CONTINUED MY WALK
BETWEEN THE MIST...
I THOUGHT ABOUT
STRANGE LOVES;
IN THE LIES...
IN WHAT MAKES
YOU SUFFER
AND CRY;
FOR PROMISED THINGS.
IT IS PLEASANT
TO BREATHE,
LAUGH, DREAM...
AND ENJOY LIFE!
I WATCHED MY STEPS...
UNDER THE COLD MOON
THAT IN THE NIGHT
SHE FOLLOWED ME;
AND NOTHING ELSE
HAPPENED...
JUST THAT
WEIRD NIGHTMARE;

WHAT COULD HAVE BEEN...
DEFINITIVE DISAPPEARANCE;
BECAUSE
SHE LOOKED AT ME...
AND I DIDN'T SEE HER;
SHE CALLED ME AND
I DID NOT HEAR HER;
SHE WHISTLED AT ME
AND I DIDN'T GO.
BECAUSE...
I WANTED TO WAIT...
FOR A BEAUTIFUL DEATH.

*

"FATAL DECLARATION"

NO! DON'T PITY ME;
DON'T LOOK AT ME
WITH SADNESS;
DON'T SAY WHAT
YOUR SOUL THINKS;
WHEN LISTENING
TO MY CONFESSION;
WHAT I FEEL
IN MY HEART
AND IN MY
DESTROYED LIFE;
THAT I CANNOT
BE LOVED,
HOW I LOVE YOU.
AND I SEE IN
YOUR REFLECTION,
WHAT YOUR EYES SAY
AND EXPRESS;
THAT YOU FEEL SORRY,
IMMENSE SORRY,
LISTEN TO MY DECLARATION
FOR NOT
FEELING THE PASSION,
HOW I FEEL FOR YOU.
BUT I DO NOT CARE
YOU'RE DENIAL;
JUST BY SEEING AND
HEARING YOU
YOUR CRYSTALLINE WORDS;
I CALM THIS
INFINITE UNFORTUNATE;

OF MY UNRETURNED LOVE;
AND VERY STAYING, BUT
NOT SURRENDERED;
I WILL CONTINUE
TO LOVE YOU MORE...
EVEN IF YOU NEVER LISTEN,
FROM MY LIPS A COMPLAINT;
AND MY HEART THAT WAITS,
WHEN PRESENTING ALL THIS;
IT WILL REMAIN, AS ALWAYS,
SAD AND HAPPY;
WITH HIS HAPPY LAUGHTER
ON THE OUTSIDE;
AND
HIS ETERNAL CRY INSIDE.

*

"NINE MONTHS"

NINE MONTHS OF AFRAID
WAITING FOR THE LOVE
THAT FINALLY ARRIVED
AFTER TO SUFFER
AND CRY
FOR SO LONG WAIT.
NINE MONTHS OF SUPPORT
THAT LARGE SENTENCE
WHERE THE DESPERATE SOUL
BEGIN TO DREAM
UNDER THE FULL MOON.
NINE MONTHS TO SEE
THE BORN OF ANOTHER HEART
THAT WILL BRING US ITS SMILE
AND IT'S INNOCENCE BEAUTY.
A NEW AWAKE
IN THE SERENE NIGHT.
A BEGIN OF LIFE THAT
IS GOING TO GROW UP
UNDER THE STARS.
NINE MONTHS ONLY
FOR THE FLOWER
THAT NICE ARRIVE
TO PERFUME
THE CHARMER
SOUL
OF THE LOVE
THAT AWAKE.

*

"THE STONE"

WHY THAT DAMN STONE
GO IN THE WAY OF
OUR PATH OF LOVE?
WHY DID SHE NOT CONTINUE
HER EXTRAVAGANT COURSE?
LOSING IT IN THE TUMULT
OF VALUELESS STONES
WHY DIDN'T THE WIND SINK HER
INTO A DEEP LAGOON?
IF YOUR SOUL WAS PURE,
LIKE THE WATER OF A SPRING
AND THAT STONE WITHOUT MERCY
STAINED YOUR FOAM WITH MUD.
WHY DID IT NOT FADE AWAY?
BEFORE MEET YOU
WHY DID IT GIVE ME
THAT PUNISHMENT?
WHY DID IT BRING ME PAIN?
WHY DID IT SHINE FOR YOU?
LIKE IT WAS A DIAMOND
IF I WAS THE BRILLIANT
THAT POSSESSED YOUR HEART.
YOU SEE YOUR STONE OF EVIL
HOW THIS LOVE MARTYRED.
LOSE YOU BY A STONE, NO!
I DECEIVED MYSELF,
I CAN'T LOSE YOU LIKE THIS...
IF YOU KNEW HOW I SUFFERED...
IF YOU KNEW HOW IT HURT ME.
A STONE WITHOUT COLOR
IN A COLD MORNING,

IT'S NOT A FANTASY
TO RELIEVE LONELINESS;
IT IS NOT VANITY EITHER,
NEITHER TENDERNESS,
NOR PLEASURE;
YOU TOOK IT
WITHOUT WANTING TO
AND YOU
SHOWED OFF WITH HER
AS IF IT WAS A STAR
THAT IS BORN AT DAWN;
YOU TOOK IT WITHOUT KNOWING,
WHICH IS SOMETHING DIRTY...
AND MEANT...
WHAT IS LIKE CUTTING A PINE
AT THE BIRTH OF SPRING;
WHICH IS A BAD WEED, CREEPER,
FULL OF SHARP THORNS...
TALKING TO YOU ABOUT CHICKS,
COVERERING YOU WITH A MANTLE...
AND MY CRY OVERFLOWED,
WHEN SEEING HER NEXT TO YOU
AS IF IT WAS AN IVY;
I LOOKING FOR YOU....
AND YOU WITH
A DIRTY STONE!

*

Havana. May 1969

"HEALTHY COUNSEL".

EAT WHAT YOU CAN;
GO WHERE YOU WANT;
LOOK AT WHAT
YOU ARE LOOKING FOR;
AND WALK.
SING IF YOU WANT;
SEE WHAT YOU HAVE;
SAY WHAT YOU FEEL;
AND WALK.
TAKE CARE OF YOUR HEART;
WITH MUSIC AND PASSION;
RELIEVE YOUR FEAR
AND WALK.
GO TO YOUR DOCTOR
IF YOU HAVE ANY PAIN
BREATHE WITH YOUR
WHOLE LUNGS
AND WALK.
DON'T SUFFER FOR LOVE
THIS IS THE BEST ADVICE
WHAT I GIVE YOU TODAY.
DO THINGS
DEVOTEDLY
AND WALK.

*

"NEW SMILE"

I AM VERY HAPPY
WHEN I SEE YOU;
IT IS NOT WEIRD,
MAY MY LOVE SMILE
FOR YOU;
IN THIS CENTURY
WHERE WITH
WE CAN SOME VALUE
GET TO KNOW
TOGETHER
A NEW COLOR
FOR OUR LIVES;
WHEN YOU ARE
NOT WORKING;
ON YOUR DAYS OFF,
THINK THAT I
I'M THINKING OF YOU...
AND CALL ME...
BECAUSE WE COULD
GET TO
KNOW TOGETHER
A NEW SMILE
FOR OUR LOVE.

*

"GREEN WAIT".

LET'S SEE WHICH OF
THE TWO...
IT IS MORE INTERESTING...
YOUR SOUL WITH ME;
MY SOUL WITH YOU;
COMPRESSING THE SENSES
WE FORM STRONG THOUGHTS;
MAKING THEM IS
THE DIFFICULT THING,
IN THIS WORLD OF DREAMS.
WITH THE COMMON HOPE
OF FINDING US
SOMETHING GOOD;
WE SURVIVE DAILY,
KILLING OTHER TIMES
FROM THE SAD PAST.
WHEN THE GREEN BLOOMS
OF WITHER HOPE,
LOVE ALSO COMES
TO HEAL OUR WOUNDS.

*

"OPEN BLOCKS"

THEY ARE OPEN BLOCKS,
OF ALL THAT IT HAD
A TIME AND IT CLOSED
FOR MORE THAN
HALF A CENTURY.
OF ALL THOSE YEARS,
WHAT WERE IN LIFE
AND SUDDENLY
THEY STAYED
SLEEPING FOR TIME
UNDEFINED;
BEING ALMOST FORGOTTEN.
MANY LOST GENERATIONS
WORSE THAN
THE HOLOCAUST.
WHO KILLED JEWS IN
CONCENTRATED FIELDS.
AND THE UNHAPPY WHO DIED
IN CRUEL WARS THAT LASTED
MANY WASTED YEARS.
THEY ARE OPEN BLOCKS TODAY;
ALL OVER THE NET AND THE WEB;
FOR THE NEW DEVELOPMENTS...
AND THEY WILL STILL BE OPEN
MORE THAN EVER NOW,
BROUGHT INTO THE WORLD
FROM THE DEEPEST
FROM THE TRUNK OF THE WISE;
THEY ARE OPEN BLOCKS
WAKE UP NOW
AND THE DUST IS REMOVED

OF TIMES PAST;
THEY LIVE AGAIN LIKE NEW
AFTER SLEEP;
AND THEY ARE PROJECTED
TO THE SUN, TO THE MOON,
TO THE SKY TO THE BREEZE
TO THE SEA,
TO THE COUNTRYSIDE.
FREE BLOCKS ARE FORMED
TRUE INFORMATION
OF FIGHT AND SONGS.
DIGITALIZED CYBERNETICS
THEY ARE OPEN BLOCKS
FOR CIVILIZED PEOPLE
IN THIS NEW CENTURY
MORE COMMUNICATIVE
WITH THE NEW
SOCIAL NETWORKS.
BY MODERN COMPUTERS
AND THE PRACTICAL LAPTOPS
AND SO
SMART CELLULAR PHONES
WE CAN ENJOY ALMOST
ALL OF THE BEST OF
THESE ADVANCED YEARS
HAS TO PROVIDE.
IN THIS CENTURY 21.

*

"TO MY LIFE"

I WOULD LIKE
TO MEET YOU
BECAUSE I WANT
ENJOY TOGETHER
BEAUTIFUL MOMENTS ...
I WOULD LIKE TO HAVE
YOU WITH ME
BECAUSE I WANT
TO LOVE YOU;
HUG YOU TIGHTLY,
THEY ARE PASSIONATE...
WITH TENDERNESS UNDER
THE SEXUAL SKIN...
FORGETTING TIME.
FULL OF SENSUALITY,
IN OUR SECRET SPACE.
FOR OUR IDYL OF LOVE.
ALSO;
I WANT FROM YOUR
BEAUTIFUL MOUTH
DRINK FROM
THE FOUNTAIN
SACRED OF KISSES
OF THE SUBLIME
DIVINITY.
FROM THE SOURCE OF
YOUR BURNING
SKIN STUCK TO MINE.
FOR MY LIFE YOU AND I
BE HAPPY.
I WOULD LIKE TO TALK

TO YOU ABOUT
FREE LOVE;
FROM THE 60's and 70'S
OF PEACE AND FAITH.
OF ROSES, WITHOUT WARS.
I WOULD LIKE TO HAVE YOU
IN MY BED OF FLOWERS;
BE UNITED, LIVE HAPPY;
I WOULD LIKE TO TAKE YOU...
TO THE DEEP FORMATION
WARMLY SEXUAL OF
THE FLESH;
INTIMIDATE, FEEL YOU,
DEVOUR YOU,
ENJOY THE NECTAR OF
YOUR SWEETNESS...
PENETRATE YOUR SECRETS...
SHARE OUR FEELINGS.
FOR MY LIFE,
FOR OUR LIVES;
FOR IN THIS WORLD
WE LIVE IN
WE BOTH BE HAPPY
UNTIL WE DIE.

*

"SWINDLE"

OH, THOSE
DAMN SCAMMERS!
OH, TO THOSE
WHO WERE SCAMMED!
WHO DO NOT KNOW
THE BEGUILE;
SO THEY WERE SCAMMED;
THERE ARE SO MANY FORMS
OF RIP-OFF
MANY ARE NEW, INVENTED;
AS I REMEMBER POE...
HE WAS THE ONE WHO
HAD WARNED US;
FEW WILL HAVE READ IT;
FEW WOULD HAVE
REMEMBERED HIM.
DAMN THOSE SWINES ARE
WHO PRACTICE THE SWINDLE
THEY WILL BE CURSED
FOR THEIR WICKEDNESS
FOR THE EVIL BORN
AND MALICE ;
THE UNHAPPY SUFFERING
PEOPLE THAT WERE
VILELY DECEIVED;
THEY WILL APPEAL TO JUSTICE,
TO BE THE CASTIGATED SCAMMER.
AND THEY WILL LEARN TO LIVE
WITHOUT EVER BEING
SCAMMED AGAIN;

IT IS THE SCAM WORSE
THAN THE THIEF
THAT STEALS
FROM THE SHAMELESS.

*

"THERE ARE BEINGS"

THERE ARE BEINGS
WHO DO NOT DESERVE
MAY ONE LOVE THEM;
BECAUSE THEY WILL NEVER FEEL
EVERYTHING WE FEEL FOR THEM.
THEY ARE LOST CASES...
IF YOU DEMAND WITH THAT
OF SACRIFICING YOUR TIME,
LEAVING BEHIND...
OTHER FEELINGS
FOR THE ALLUSIVE ATTEMPTS;
IT WILL WEIGH YOU LATER.
THAT YOU HAVE TOLD THEM.
THERE ARE BEINGS
WHO DO NOT DESERVE
THAT ONE WANTS THEM
BECAUSE
THEY ARE EMPTY BEINGS.
IF YOU PERSIST IN YOUR TRY
LOVING...
LEAVING OTHERS WHO ARE
LOOKING TO RECEIVE
THAT BEAUTIFUL LOVE
ROMANTIC, DREAMED, LONGED
WHAT ARE YOU GIVING TO A LOST,
YOU WILL REGRET IT LATER
WHEN IT'S TOO LATE NOW
AND IN THE END
YOU UNDERSTAND;

IT'S NOT WORTH
SUFFERING SO MUCH
FOR A BEING WHO
DOES NOT FEEL THE SAME.

*

"MY SOUL"

TAKE CARE OF
YOUR SOUL;
FILL IT WITH LOVE
DON'T MIST HER
LOVE HER MORE
THAN YOURSELF!
LOVE HER
WITH PASSION!
THE TIMES I HAVE
NOT PAID ATTENTION
TO MY ENCHANTED SOUL;
THIS IS WHEN I HAVE
MADE MISTAKES
THEY HAVE
WEIGHED ME THEN.
I WAS STILL VERY YOUNG;
I DIDN'T KNOW
HOW TO GUIDE ME
WHEN MAKING
SERIOUS DECISIONS;
THAT'S WHY NOW
I AM GUIDED BY
MY SOUL;
AND I FEEL SAFE
OF MY ACTIONS.
THE SOUL ALWAYS SAYS
WHAT IS BEST TO LIVE
IN THESE TIMES
OF UNCERTAINTY
WHERE WE
DON'T KNOW

IF WE ARE ALIVE
WE WILL DAWN
WHEN WE WAKE UP
TOMORROW.
DIVINE SOUL,
ENCHANTED SOUL
THANKS TO YOU
I AM ALIVE TODAY.

*

"WHEN WAKENING UP"

EVERY DAY FOR
THOSE OF US WHO ARE
HERE STILL BREATHING,
ON THIS PLANET
WHERE WE LIVE;
INHABITANTS OF THE EARTH;
EACH ONE, INDIVIDUAL AND
UNIQUE IN YOUR LIFE,
IN ITS EXCLUSIVE SPACE,
WITH TIME COUNTED
IN HIS PERSONAL EXISTENCE...
EACH ONE WITH HIS STORY;
WITH THE PRESENT SITUATION,
WITH HIS GLORY
OR WITH HIS HELL;
YOU HAVE TO ACCEPT
THE CURRENT REALITY
EFFECTIVE WITH COURAGE
AND WITHOUT FEAR.
AND CONFORM
WITHOUT PROTESTING
WITH THE BEAUTIFUL
OR UGLY HOURS
OF THE NEW DAY...
TO CONTINUE...
EVERYONE WITH
THE ACTION
AND
THE DIGITAL MOVEMENT,
DEPENDING
ON THE CELL PHONE

IN EVERY MINUTE OR INSTANT
WHAT WE HAVE IN
THE CHALLENGE OF
THE STRUGGLE FOR LIFE;
WHEN YOU WAKE UP
YOU ARE ALIVE
AND CONSCIOUS;
ONE MORE TEST OF
YOUR RESISTANCE
PHYSICAL AND MENTAL;
SINCE YOU GET UP
TO THE MEETING OF THE SUN.
DON'T FORGET THAT YOU LIVE.
YOU EXIST AND
YOU ARE THE OWNER
ABSOLUTE OF YOUR PERSON
LIKE EARTH, LIKE
HUMAN.
WE ARE BORN FOR GOOD,
AND WE ARE CONDEMNED
FOR EVIL.
THE SUBLIME LOVE
OF THE HEALTHY HEART
SAVES US.
IT IS THE GRACE OF HEAVEN.
WE RECEIVE IT AND INHERIT IT
FROM OTHER GOOD SOULS,
BECAUSE WE LOVE
EACH OTHER
AND WE KNOW
HOW TO LOVE,
BY DENTIGUING WISELY
OF GOOD AND EVIL.

*

"MY LONELINESS"

I KNOW MY LONELINESS,
WHEN CROSS BY MY SIDE,
THIS BITTER REALITY,
THAT HAS US SEPARATED;
LIVE LIKE THIS... CHAINED;
IT IS FILLED WITH FEAR;
IT IS SUFFERING
FROM ANGUISH
TORMENT YOURSELF;
IT IS FILLED WITH GENTLE.
LIKE A DROWNED CRY;
LIKE ENDURING PAIN,
LIKE SUFFERING
A PENALTY;
AS TIED TO LOVE;
LIKE FEELING YOUR KISSES;
LIKE FEELING ILLUSION...
ALONE WITH MY
DISCONSOLATION;
ONLY WITH MY PASSION;
ONLY WITH YOUR MEMORY
AND ONLY WITH MY CRY.
DON'T GIVE ME
ANY MORE AGONY;
I FEEL A LOT OF FEAR
LOSE YOU MY LIFE....
IT IS LOSING MY HEART;
DON'T LEAVE ME
ALONE MY LOVE
DO NOT GO PLEASE;
I ALREADY FEEL THE COLD

THAT YOUR
SHADOW LEFT ME.
AND HAVE YOU
BETWEEN MY ARMS...
I CAN NOT ANYMORE;
SUFFERING YOUR
INCOMPREHENSION;
ALONE WITH
MY DISCOUNT;
ALONE WITH MY PAIN;
ONLY WITH YOUR MEMORY
AND ONLY WITH MY SONG.

*

"CINEMA"

I LOVE CINEMA
AND ALL MOVIES;
THE SILENT, CLASSIC
AND MODERN;
THOSE OF ACTION,
THOSE OF WAR,
THOSE OF CULT,
THOSE OF HORROR,
THOSE
OF SCIENCE FICTION,
THOSE OF MYSTERY,
SUSPENSE, DRAMAS
AND COMEDIES.
THE SUREALISTIC,
THE NON-REALIST,
THE FILM NOIR,
THE PSYCODELICS, AND
THE EXISTENTIALISTS.
THOSE OF VAMPIRES,
THOSE OF MONSTERS
AND THOSE OF FANTASIES.
SINCE
THE CINEMATOGRAPH BEGAN
MORE THAN A CENTURY AGO
I WAS CAPTIVED BY CINEMA.
THAT'S WHY I LOVE IT
SO MUCH SINCE I WAS A CHILD.
IT TRANSPORTS ME,
EDUCATES ME
AND MAKES ME HAPPY.
IT HAS BEEN THE MAIN

CULTURE OF THE PEOPLES,
OF THE ILLITERATES, OF THE WISE.
I LOVE CINEMASCOPE,
COLOR OF LUXES,
PANAVISÓN, TECHNICOLOR,
METROCOLOR, BLACK AND WHITE,
SEPIA, CINERAMA, PANORAMIC
AND THIRD DIMENSION.
AND NOW CINEMA HAS
DEVELOPED MORE THAN EVER;
THE SEVENTH ART OF THE NEW TIMES;
IT IS SUPER EVOLVED IN ITS DIGITALIZED
CINEMATOGRAPHIC MAGNIFICENCE
OF THIS CENTURY.
THAT WONDER CREATED
BY THE HUMAN MIND;
HAS MADE GREAT ADVANCES
INTO THE FUTURE
THAT UNION OF WORLD CINEMA
WITH ALL COUNTRIES.
THAT DIVINE GRACE OF KNOWING
ALL THE ARTS COMBINED
IN ONE FACET: MUSIC,
DRAMA, COMEDY,
PAINTINGS AND ALL KINDS
OF INTERESTING PLOTS
AND WONDERFUL STORIES.
MASTERPIECES OF
THE HUMAN BEING;
THEY HAVE EMERGED AND
HAVE LASTED THANKS
TO CINEMA.
ALL THE COUNTRIES
THAT MAKE MOVIES,

THEY MAKE THEM KNOWN AND
WE CAN ABOUT THEM
KNOW HOW THINGS
ARE ON THE PLANET.
INTERNATIONAL FILM FESTIVALS
ABOVE ALL THEY
ARE VERY IMPORTANT;
BEING ABLE TO SEE AND KNOW
ABOUT SO MANY NEW THINGS.
I LOVE CINEMA, WE LOVE
THE DIRECTORS, THE PRODUCERS,
AND
THE PROTAGONISTS.
BUT MOST OF ALL
TO THE FAMOUS
HOLLYWOOD STARS.
THROUGH CINEMA WE KNOW
FOR CERTAIN SCIENCE;
WHAT NO ONE HAS EVER TOLD US.
ETERNAL GLORY TO CINEMA;
INVENTION OF THE 20TH CENTURY
DIGITALIZED IN THE 21ST CENTURY.
CELLULOID SUPREMACY
FROM THE WIDE AND SMALL SCREEN.
HOLLYWOOD WITH ITS OSCARS,
IS MECCA.
SPAIN WITH ITS GOYAS
AND FRANCE WITH THE CESARS
THE OTHER COUNTRIES WITH
THE GOLDEN PALM,
THE SILVER BEAR, ECT.
WHICH HAVE GAINED A LOT OF
INTERNATIONAL PRESTIGE.
THANKS TO CINEMA AT ALL TIMES

LIVED AND WILL CONTINUE TO LIVE;
INCREASINGLY MORE INNOVATIVE
AND PLEASANT.
I LOVE CINEMA A LOT,
I LOVE MOVIES.
LONG LIVE THE CINEMA,
MAY IT NEVER DIE.

*

"TO JOSE MARTI"!

APOSTLE OF CUBA;
INTELLECTUAL OF THE SOUL;
THANKS TO YOU CUBANS
WE FREED US FROM SPAIN
AND YOU INHERITED US
YOUR CULTURE;
YOUR EXAMPLE,
YOUR BOOKS, YOUR IDEALS
AND YOUR LOVE
FOR THE COUNTRY.
WE FEEL PROUD
FOR YOUR GREATNESS OF SOUL.
LEAVE US THE SOCIAL LEGACY,
POLITICAL AND
CULTURAL BEAUTIFUL
OF FREEDOM.
THE GREATEST THINKER
WHAT CUBA HAS GIVEN.
READ EVERYONE
HIS MASTERPIECES:
THE GOLDEN AGE, FOR
CHILDREN AND ADULTS,
HIS ESSAYS AND POEMS;
HIS POLITICAL WRITINGS;
MARTI'S THOUGHTS
BUT, ABOVE ALL
DON'T STOP READING
HIS SIMPLE VERSES.
LIKE THIS BEAUTIFUL VERSE
"I come from all over"
And everywhere I go

I am art among arts
And on the mountain,
I am a mountain"
SOME OF THEM CHOSEN
PETER SEEGER TO SING
"LA GUANTANAMERA".
WHICH STARTED LIKE THIS:
"I am an honest man
where the palm grows from;
and before I die I want,
cast my verse from the soul."
OH! MARTI, MY MASTER,
WONDERFUL SPIRITUAL GUIDE
OF MY INTELLECT.
I CARRY YOU FOREVER
IN THE MOST REMEMBER
PURE AND SINCERE THAT I KEEP
IN MY HEART.

*

"AIDS"

IT IS A CRUEL DISEASE
THAT MAKES YOU WANT TO CRY
TO THOSE WHO HAVE TO SUFFER IT;
BECAUSE IT IS REALLY
A TERRIBLE AGONY;
YOU HAVE TO SEE IT SERIOUSLY
SO NO ONE LAUGHS.
IT'S A SAD AND EVIL THING
THAT CANNOT BE CURE;
IT'S A MACABRE BRAND
THAT NO ONE CAN TAKE AWAY.
IT IS THE CURSE THAT PUNISHES,
TO THOSE WHO WERE
NOT PROTECTED
AT THE TIME OF ENJOYING.
A DIFFICULT CALAMITY;
WHAT CAN CONTAGATE YOU
IF YOU DON'T TAKE CARE
OF YOURSELF WELL,
THAT LIMITS YOU TO WAITING
IN DEFINITIVE DESPERATION,
WHAT SHOULD BE CONTROLLED,
WITH PASSIVE RESIGNATION.
IT IS THE TIP OF THE THORN
THAT FORESTERS UNTIL IT KILLS
TO THE INNOCENT VICTIM
WHAT ANXIOUSLY WAITING FOR
THE CURE OF THIS EVIL
TO PROLONG LIFE.

*

"TO THE CUBAN PAINTER RENATO MARTINEZ PEÑA." (1953-2016)

HAS THE NOBILITY OF THE PRINCE
HIS WORKS ARE THE BEAUTIES
OF THE ROYAL PALACE.
HE PAINTS TO JOY,
THE VIEW OF THE DISTRACTED.
PAINT FOR YOUR FRIENDS...
AND FOR THOSE WHO
WANT TO APPRECIATE IT.
HE DOES NOT WISH
TO REFLECT
WHAT IS SAD
OR WHAT IS DEPRESSING.
ALWAYS WORK SMILING
WHEN HE GIVEN TO PAINT.
WE CANNOT DETECT
WHICH OF YOUR PAINTINGS
IS THE MOST BEAUTIFUL.
EVERYONE HAS THE SEAL
OF HIS SIDERAL MAGIC.
HIS PAINTINGS MAKE US
REMEMBER
THEMES OF BEAUTIFUL SONGS.
JOY THE HEARTS
AND IT MAKES US SIGH.
WITH ANGELICAL TENDERNESS
CREATE THE FLOWERS
OF PARADISE.
WITH BLESSED ENTHUSIASM
PARTY BUTTERFLIES FLY;

CONFUSING THE FOREST
WITH ITS RANGE OF COLORS.
RHYTHMICALLY COMPOSES
TO THE TONE OF NATURE.

*

"LOVING FOR NOTHING"

AFTER LIVING SO LONG TOGETHER,
WITHOUT KISSES, OR CARESSING;
NOTHING MUTUAL...
WAITING FOR
THE PASSIONAL MEETING
OF LOVE IN DELIGHTS,
LOVING FOR NOTHING!
WITHOUT
RECEIVING WARM HUGS,
ONLY UNFAIR PAINS,
SADNESS, DISAPPOINTMENTS,
DEEP HOLD.
GIVING WITHOUT RECEIVING
NOTHING IN EXCHANGE,
ONLY UNFAIR MISTREATMENT;
YOU GOT USED TO ME
TO BEAR YOUR REJECTION
TO LIVE IN YOUR RARE WORLD.
AND IN THE END AFTER ALL
YOU WENT IN ANOTHER COURSE.
AND NOW THAT YOU LEFT ME,
I WOULD LIKE TO BELONG TO THE
OF RIGHTEOUS HEARTS.
NO TO THE LOW OF HEART,
NOR TO CORRUPT BEINGS.
BEFORE DEMOTING MYSELF
TO ANOTHER
NEW WANT,
WISHING YOUR BODY,
I PREFER TO LIVE FOREVER
IN THE LONELINESS;

KEEPING MY LOVE PURE.
I WILL STAY HERE FORGETTING YOU,
I WILL CONTINUE LIKE THIS
TO SAVE MYSELF FROM DIE;
WITHOUT SURRENDERING MYSELF
IN BODY AND SOUL
TO NO ONE EVER,
NEVER AGAIN TO ANYONE
I WILL GET IN...
LOVING FOR NOTHING.

July 01, 1990

*

"WAKEFULNESS"

AT NIGHT ...
WHEN THE DARKNESS CAUSES
PHANTOMY SHADOWS,
AROUND MY BED
WHERE THE TULES SHIVE
BY THE PITYLESS WIND,
AND THE CRICKETS MOAN
AND SING
THEIR VIOLENT HYMNS;
I DON'T FEEL SLEEPY!
AT NIGHT ...
WHEN EVERYTHING
SEEMS TO DIE
UNDER THE BLACK SKY,
AND EVERYTHING SEEMS TO BE...
THE SIGN OF DISCONSOLATION,
I DON'T FEEL SLEEPY!
AT NIGHT ...
WHEN THE MOON PENETRATES
THROUGH MY OPEN WINDOW
AND A SCENARIO IS MADE
OF SHADOWS...
THE RESTLESS LIGHT
OF SCARY ...
I WANT TO SCREAM!
TO THE FOUR WINDS!
CRYING FOR A LOVE...
LET IT KILL MY DEATH...
I DON'T FEEL SLEEPY!
I DON'T FEEL SLEEPY!
AND FROM MY INSIDE

A VOICE COMES OUT
THAT CAN MORE
THAN SILENCE;
AND SCREAMS
FULL OF BURNING;
A NAKED, FEBRILE BODY!
BEAUTIFUL, SLIM!
LET ME ENVELOPE IN YOUR SKIN,
LET ME DRUNK WITH KISSES,
MAY FILL ME WITH HUGS;
LET MY DESIRES CALM ME;
DELIVERED TO PLEASURE
TO ENJOY BOTH...
HAPPY IN THE BED;
TO EMBRACE ME TOO,
TO TIGHTEN ME STRONGLY
AGAINST MY CHEST,
TO BE ABLE TO FEEL
THE INTIMATE FEELING
OF SEXUAL PLEASURE...
MELTED IN A SINGLE KISS.
UNTIL IT FINALLY SPREADS
OUT OF ME!
LIKE A VOLCANO OF FIRE!
THE REFULGENT FLARE
INSIDE THE HEAT
OF MY BODY!
AND MY EYES FLASH!
AND
IT CONVULSES MY BRAIN!
UNTIL EVERYTHING...
BE CALM;
PASS AND DISAPPEAR
MY MEMORY....

CALMING DOWN LIKE THIS...
ALSO MY WISH.
AND MY EVIL IS RELIEVED,
THOUGHT IS DESTROYED...
I CLOSE MY EYES FINALLY;
AFTER A LONG SILENCE,
I SLEEP QUIET NOW,
I WILL NOT WAKE UP
FOR A MOMENT;
I HAVE BEEN SURRENDERED,
SURRENDERED!
LIKE A DEAD MAN;
AND WHEN
THE DAWN COMES,
I ONLY KNOW
THAT I WOKE UP!

*

"HALLOWEEN 1982"

THE BIG HOUSE OF HAPPY CATS
LOCATED
at 1315 STEVENSON STREET,
IN S.F.
RECEIVED AT 11:55 P.M.
THE NIGHT MYSTERY
OF THE APPEARANCE OF
A BEAUTIFUL FAIRY
THAT NO ONE HAD EVER SEEN
IN NO CHILDREN'S STORY.
SWEETENED WITH HONEY
PUMPKINS MADE FACES
HAPPY, DEVIL AND SAD,
OF THE MAGICAL NIGHT OF
LAST DAY OF
THE MONTH OCTOBER,
AT THE EXOTIC PARTY
COSTUMES AND
HORRIBLE MASKS;
AND ALL THE FELINES
IN THE NEIGHBORHOOD
THEY WERE VERY HAPPY,
AND THEY BECAME
MORE ECCENTRIC
HAPPY DANCING,
ENJOYING
FROM THAT
SUBLIME MOMENT.
IT HAD BEEN
THE OLD WITCH LILLY,
THAT AT THE END

OF HER EXPERIMENTS
TO REACH
THE BIZARRE POWER
NOT TO AGE, OR DIE,
SHE FINALLY FOUND THE SPELL
THAT TRANSFORMED HER INTO A
BEAUTIFUL GOOD FAIRY...
AND WAS
THE CROWNED QUEEN,
THAT UNFORGETTABLE
HALLOWEEN NIGHT.

*

"PRAYER TO THE WATER."

HOLY AND
POWERFUL WATER!
ADORABLE WATER,
PURE WATER!
PROTECTIVE WATER!
GOOD WATER!
CLEAN AND CRYSTAL
CLEAR WATER!
BLESSING AND
BEAUTIFUL WATER!
INEXHAUSTIBLE SPRING
OF PURIFYING ENERGY.
RAIN WATER! SEAWATER!
WATER FROM RIVERS
AND STREAMS!
LIGHT-SAVING WATER!
PROTECT US FROM ALL EVIL;
OF EVERY EVIL.
CLEANSE US FROM ANY SPELL,
OF ALL EVIL;
OF ALL BASENESS
AND HUMILIATION.
FREE ME FROM ANY INJUSTICE,
THAT IT IS INTENDED
TO EXERCISE OVER ME.
HOLY WATER!
BEAUTIFUL WATER!
FLOWER WATER,
FRESH WATER,
DIVINE WATER,
MAGIC WATER,

DISCOVER YOUR POWER
OVER US
WE LOVE YOU FULL
OF GRATITUDE
FOR YOUR IMPRESSIVE SERVICE
OF PURE AND
BEAUTIFUL LOVE
LIKE YOUR TRANSPARENTS
DEW DROPS EVERY DAWN.
HEAVENLY WATER!
FLORIDA WATER!
WATER
FROM THE FOUNTAINS!
STRONG WATER!
VIRGIN WATER!
GODDESS WATER!
FRIENDLY WATER!
SWEET WATER!
FROZEN WATER!
WARM WATER!
HOT AND COLD WATER!
DEFEND US FROM
PERVERSITY,
OF OUR ENEMIES,
OF THE ENVIOUS,
AND WRONG
AND GIVE BACK
WITH GROWTH
TO THE EVIL
AND THE VILLAINS
HIS VILE EVIL.
IMMENSE WATER,
FULL OF POWER!
SUNLIGHT

ENCHANTED WATER!
THANK YOU THANK YOU
VERY MUCH!
FOR YOUR
WONDERFUL PROTECTION.
AMEN.

*

"THE DANGER"

DANGEROUSLY WE LIVING
BEINGS ON EARTH;
UNDER THE SAME SKY
WHERE WE ARE
BORN IGNORANTS
FIGHTING DAILY
TO SURVIVE
EACH DAY
TO PAY FOR OUR
HUMAN EXISTENCE
WITH MONEY.
THE PEOPLE MIND
IS LITTLE PREPARED
TO BELIEVE IT;
PREGNANT WITH SO
MANY FEELINGS
FROM THE HEART.
SCIENCE HARDENS
WITHOUT FANTASIES,
AND THE STATISTICS FIT
TO THE REASON.
A BULL CAN CHARGE
TO A CHILD RIDING
ON A WOODEN
ROCKING HORSE.
A CAR BY ACCIDENT
CAN ALSO
RUN DOWN ON THE STREET
TO AN INNOCENT CYCLIST
MOUNTED ON HIS BIKE.
WARS AND HUNGER

CONTINUE IN MANY COUNTRIES,
BOTH ARE KILLING
WITHOUT COMPASSION
TO MANY BEINGS
IN THIS WORLD;
AND THE ESCAPISM WITH
ALCOHOL AND DRUGS
USE SOME RECKLE GROUPS
TO BE OUT OF THE HARD
REALITY
OF THE IMMENSE UNIVERSE.
TRANSPORTING THEYSELF
TO ANOTHER
VERY FAR DIMENSION.
AFECTED, IN CONFLICT ARE
MANY DESPERATE SOULS
LOOKING FOR THE SOLUTION
TO THE MISTAKES COMMITED
WITHOUT MEANING TO
OR WANTING TO DO IT.
THERE EXISTS UNKNOWN
DESTINATION FOR EACH
ONE IN THIS WORLD;
WITH TWO
FUNDAMENTAL CODES;
TWO POLES, TWO CREEDS,
TWO PATHS TO CHOOSE FROM;
WHICH WILL DETERMINE
THE REST OF YOURS DAYS
FOREVER,
EVERY DAY UNTIL THE END
OF LIFE.
THEY ARE ACCORDING
THEIR MORALE

DON'T DO ANYTHING WRONG.
WE KNOW THAT EXIST
HIDDEN SECRETS
THAT WE NEVER WILL KNOW
AND THEY WILL GO AWAY
WITH THOSE
WHO KEPT THEM IN.
SOMEONE SAID
THERE ARE BEINGS FROM
OTHER PLANETS
ACCLIMATIZED ON
THIS EARTH
SINCE THE BEGINNING OF
THE HUMAN EXISTENCE
THEY CAN NOT BE DISOVERED
BECAUSE THEY DIE.
MANY OF THEM
ARE SUSPECTED
TO BE THOSE CELEBRATED
ARTISTS AND INVENTORS
WHO DID SOMETHING
EXTRAORDINARY AS:
LEONARDO DA VINCI,
VERNE, DISNEY AND
MANY MORE.
ELECTRONIC COMPUTERS ARE
ALREADY BEING INVENTED,
TO CREATE THE
ARTIFICIAL INTELLIGENCY
OF THE NEXT CENTURY.
BUT IT STILL KEEPS WARNING US
OF THE DANGER THE SAME
ANIMAL INSTINCT,
THAT WE HAVE THE INHABITANTS

OF OUR PLANET EARHT
THE THIRD OF THE
SOLAR SYSTEM.
WE ALL TRY TO AVOID DANGERS
WHENEVER WE SEE IT LATENTS
BECAUSE EXIST DEATH AND
EVERYTHING ENDS
IN THE WORLD.
WE COMBATING
THE DANGER
TO AVOID DYING FOR
SOME INCCIDENTS.
IT'S THE FEAR OF DIE
WHAT WE ALL BE AFRAID
BECAUSE WE ARE ALIVE.
STILL WE NEED SPEND
THIRTYSIX SPRING MORE
TO THE END OF THE
20th. CENTURY
AND FOREVER WE PREFER
NOT TO THINK ABOUT
THE END THAT WE'LL HAVE.
WE ALL WANT TO HAVE
A BEAUTIFULL DEATH.
WE MOVE AWAY FROM
ANYTHING THAT SMELL
OF DANGER.
FLEEING FROM
DANGER IS WISE.
AND THE DANGER IS THAT
NO ONE WILL EVER KNOW
HOW WE WILL DIE.

*

Havana, Summer 1964

"DISCOVERED SOUL"

YOU DIDN'T STAND IT,
IT WAS TOO STRONG
FOR YOU.
THE PRESSURE WAS
DETESTABLE TOO;
AND YOUR LOVE
CAME TO SUFFER IT.
OLD PAINS HAD
LOCKED YOU UP
IN FEARS AND FAILURES;
INTERNAL SHOCKS,
OF LONELINESS
AND BROKENNESS.
OLD PASSIONS
OF TREMBLING
AND CRYING;
STRUGGLES, ILLUSIONS
AND REJECTIONS.
YOU WERE ON
ONE SIDE OF LIFE,
WITH CLOSED WINDOWS
AND COLD CROSSES.
SURROUNDED
BY ADVERSITY;
WRAPPED IN
THE AGONY.
SLEEPLESS NIGHTS
IN EMPTY BED;
NO CARESSING,
NO KISSING,
NO DELIGHTS.
HOPES IN THE SUN,

SADNESS, MELANCHOLY;
AND FINALLY
YOU LAUNCHED
TOWARDS THE OTHER SHORE,
BREAKING WHEN JUMPING
THE MASK THAT COVERED
YOUR NIGHTMARE;
AND ON THAT FLIGHT
YOU WERE DRIFT;
WILL YOU BE DISCOVERED
IN THE WONDER?
AND THE BITTER RITE
OF YOUR PAIN
THAT CRIED IN YOUR SMILE
IT WILL BE A FLOWER
OPEN TO LOVE
IN THIS NEW LIFE.
DESPERATE SOUL
FOR HAVING CARESSING'S,
TENDER, WARM PILLOWS;
WAIT FOR THE
TOUCH OF LOVE;
WAIT WITH DIVINE GRACE
WITH FAITH,
WITH LIVING HOPES
AND LIVE WITH THIS
BEAUTIFUL ILLUSION
THAT ESCAPES
FROM THE DARK
SUFFOCATING SHADOW,
IN THE WHITE LIGHT OF DAY
THAT WILL GIVE YOU
ANOTHER OPPORTUNITY
BETTER IN THIS OTHER LIFE.

*

"IN SEARCH OF MY GREEN UNICORN"

IT IS A DIFFICULT POSITION
STAND LIKE A HORSE;
BUT WHAT IS
A GREEN UNICORN?
HE HAS STOP ON HIS
TWO BEAUTIFUL
HIND LEGS
IN SUCH AN
ANGELICAL WAY
LIKE NO OTHER ANIMAL
IT HAS NEVER STAND UP.
WHEN I KNEW THAT,
DUE TO DIVINE OBSERVATION
WHAT DID I DO TO HIM,
I UNDERSTOOD, THEN,
THAT HE COULD DO IT EASILY;
OTHERS WILL NOT
BE ABLE TO DO IT,
EVEN IF THEY KNOW
THIS OR KNOW
LIKE HE DOES IT.
NOT EVERYONE DOES
THE SAME THING.
THERE ARE BEINGS WHO
KNOW HOW TO IMITATE
TO OTHER BEINGS AND
OTHERS CANNOT.
THERE ARE BEINGS WHO
READ A LOT

TO TRY TO WRITE A BOOK;
AND THEY NEVER DO IT.
BECAUSE THEY HAVE LIVED
WITHOUT ITS OWN STORY.
I WILL NOT BE LIKE THE CRAB
THAT FALLS ASLEEP
IN YESTERDAY;
I WILL BE LIKE THE SCORPIO
WHO ONLY THINKS
IN THE GREAT POWER.
AND...
IN SURVIVING IN ANY
DIFFICULT CIRCUMSTACE OF LIFE.
IN MY SWEET DREAMS
I WILL LOOK FOR MY BEAUTIFUL
GREEN UNICORN HOPE
THAT WILL GUIDE ME SMILING
ON THE PATHS OF BONANZAS,
ALWAYS SINGING AND RECITING
SWEET POEMS OF THE SOUL.
I WILL LISTEN TO
THE SUBLIME MELODY
OF LOVE EVERY DAY;
I WILL FORGET EVERYONE
THE DISAPPOINTMENTS
OF THE PAST
I WILL LIVE HAPPY AND JOYFUL
WITH MY GREEN UNICORN
THAT WILL NEVER BETRAY ME
AND HE WILL LOVE ME
FULL OF LOVE
FOR THE WHOLE ETERNITY
IT WILL FOREVER BE MINE
BECAUSE A LOT, A LOT

HE WILL LOVE ME!
AFTER ALL...
CRAZYS PAINTS THE UNICORN
THE COLOR THEY WANT.

*

"TO LAST ON EARTH"

IT IS THE IMPORTANCE
WE HAVE
WHEN WE REALIZE
OUR FIGHT FOR EXISTENCE
ON THIS PLANET OF
WATER, AIR
FIRE AND EARTH.
EVERYONE LIVES THEIR
LIFE AS THEY CAN
AND THAT WAY
YOU FEEL REALITY
LATENT OF
THE WORLD ALWAYS
IN THE DAMN WARS.
WE LIVE WITH HOPE
TO LAST FOR MANY YEARS
EVEN THOUGH
WE SUFFER AND CRY
FOR CRUEL DISAPPOINTMENTS.
DREAMS ARE COMPETITIVE,
AND WE ALL WANT THE BEST
THINGS BIG, BEAUTIFUL AND
THE MOST SIGNIFICANT THING...
IN THIS SACRED ERA
OF INDEFINITE TIME.
WHERE THE FORCES
OF THE MINDS
THEY WILL BE ABLE
BY AMBITION
TO DISAPPEAR
OF THE EARTH GLOBE

TO ALL HUMANITY.
AND NOTHING OF WHAT
WAS ACHIEVED
UNTIL NOW, IT WILL REMAIN
IN THIS STRANGE WORLD.
THAT'S WHY IT'S
VERY IMPORTANT
FOR THOSE SPECIAL SOULS,
TO THOSE WHO
I ADDRESS TODAY,
THAT THEY KNOW HOW
TO PLEASE GOD,
TO THE ONLY TRUE, GOD;
TO THE GOD OF
YOUR CONSCIENCES,
OF EMOTIONAL STABILITY,
AND THE JOY OF LIVING,
TO LAST ON EARTH
IN THIS TREMENDOUS YEAR,
WHERE HUMANITY ARRIVED
TO THE BAD DEGREE OF HATE
BY KNOWING CLOSELY
THE TERRORISM!
THAT HAS EMERGED FROM EVIL
FROM AN ORGANIZED GROUP
OF STRANGE EXTREMIST BEINGS
AND WICKED, DIRECTED BY
THE SANGUINARY KILLER
KADAFIR OF LIBYA.

S.F. May 11. 1986

*

"PHILOSOPHY"

THE MAN FIGHTS
FOR HUNGER AND LOVE.
LIKE AND DISLIKE
IT'S THE MENTAL DIVISION
OF HUMAN BEINGS.
AND ALL CREATURES
LIVING OF OUR PLANET.
OUR MAIN PURPOSE
IT IS TO PLEASE EVERY TASTE,
AS THEY ALWAYS PROPOSED
ALL STAR LUMINAIRES
THAT SHINE FOR THEIR
BEAUTIFUL ART
IN THIS COMPLICATED LAND.
WHAT WE DON'T LIKE
NOTIFY US SO THAT
LET'S NOT TRY IT.
BUT THE MYSTERIOUS
DESTINY OF MAN
IS THAT THINGS
THEY DON'T HAPPEN LIKE
ONE WISHES THEY HAPPENED.
AND THAT THIS GREAT TRUTH
WE ASSIMILE IT WITH
DIVINE UNDERSTANDING
SO THAT IT DOES
NOT AFFECT US
OUR DELICATE AND
SENSITIVE HEART.

*

"MOTHER"

WE ARE ALL BORN OF
A MOTHER;
AND FROM BIRTH
THE STORY WILL BEGIN
OF OUR LIFE.
BLESSED THOSE SONS
AND DAUGHTERS
THAT CAN BE CARED FOR
BY HIS BIOLOGICAL PARENTS
OR ADOCTIVE SINCE
THEY ARE BORN.
BUT MOST OF ALL F
OR THE MOTHER.
MOTHER'S LOVE IS
THE MOST IMPORTANT THING
IN A HUMAN BEING.
POOR THOSE UNHAPPY
THAT THEY GOT AN EVIL MOTHER.
LUCKY THEY ARE NOT VERY ABOUT
BECAUSE MOTHERHOOD SIMPLY IS
A DIVINE FEMALE HORMONE
THAT ALWAYS PRODUCES LOVE.
UNCONDITIONAL MATERNAL LOVE,
PURITY OF SOUL AND SWEETNESS
IN THE HEART.
BLESSED ARE THOSE
THAT THEY CAN BE EDUCATED
AND GROW
WITHIN A HAPPY FAMILY,

AND NOT IN
A DYSFUNCTIONAL ONE.
MOTHER'S DAY
IT'S EVERY DAY!

*

"PURE FEELING"

THE BIG HEARTS;
THE LITTLE HEARTS
WE MUST ALWAYS
BE UNITED
FOR THE PUREST FEELING
THAT EXISTS IN ALL OF US
LIVING BEINGS.
THAT PURE
LEGITIMATE FEELING
THAT LIVES IN OUR LIVES,
LIMITED LIFE WE HAVE
IN THIS COMPLICATED WORLD
WHERE WE HAVE TO LIVE
THE HOURS, THE MINUTES,
THE SECONDS, THE DAYS,
THE WEEKS, THE MONTHS
AND THE YEARS,
EVERY INSTANT
AT ALL TIMES;
TO FEEL THAT
SWEET PLEASURE
THAT WE ALL
CARRY INSIDE
FROM THE HEART;
THAT PURE FEELING
WHAT IS CALLED LOVE.

*

"HIDE IT"

THAT FALSE UNHEALTHY PRIDE
HIDE IT, HIDE IT WELL,
SO THAT YOU NEVER
SHOW THEM
TO NO ONE,
AND BE YOUR LOSE.
HIDE YOUR ANGER TOO,
YOUR GLUTTONY AND
YOUR AMBITION.
ALL YOUR BAD FLAWS
THAT WILL BE
YOUR DESTRUCTION.
HIDE THEM WHERE NO ONE
NEVER SEE THEM.
HIDE THEM IN YOUR HEART
HIDE YOURSELF LATER
OF FRUSTRATION
DO NOT GO OUTSIDE
EXHIBITING YOUR DEPRESSION
BECAUSE NO ONE WILL WANT
LOOK AT YOU DRAGGING
THAT CONDITION.
HIDE IT ALL
HIDE YOUR SINS WELL,
AND BE CAREFUL
OF THE CURSE.
HIDE IT, OR BETTER
BURN IT ALL,
CONVERT IT AT ONCE
IN COAL ASHES

*

"US"

EVERY 24 HOURS THERE IS
ANOTHER DAWN OF LIFE
IN EACH OF THE LIVING
OF THE PROMISED LAND.
EVERY SECOND OF
OUR TIME COUNTS
SINCE WE WOKE UP
TO SURVIVE
IN YOUR SPACE,
IN THE PLACE, IN TIME
WHERE WE HAD TO BE
BORN AND DIE.
EVERYONE WITH A MIND
ALWAYS AWAKEN
AND A HEART BEATING
TO LOVE.
EACH ONE IN
A DIFFERENT
CIRCUMSTANCE
LIVING IN
THE PRESENT MOMENT
OF ITS CURRENT TRUTH,
WITHOUT BEING
ABLE TO GO BACK.
EACH ONE WITH PATIENCE
OR IMPATIENTLY WITH
HOPE, WAITING
FOR SOMETHING
THAT MAYBE IT WILL
BE ACHIEVED.
WITH DIFFERENT

PROBLEMS TO SOLVE
IN THE SHORT TERM,
LATER OR
IMMEDIATELY.
EACH ONE SEEKING TO
LOVE AND BE LOVED
AND SOMETHING
TO EAT DAILY.
EVERYONE KNOWS WHEN
WE ARE BORN
BUT
WITHOUT KNOW WHEN
WE WILL DIE.
EVERY ONE AGING SLOWLY
FROM THE BLESSED BIRTH.
EVERY ONE IN THIS WORLD
IT HAS THE SKY FOR A ROOF
AND TO THE EARTH FOR BED.
EVERYONE HAS A MISSION
AT YOUR MARKED
DESTINATION
EVERYONE ALWAYS HAS
SOMETHING TO DO IN LIFE
WITH ITS DAYS COUNTED.
EVERYONE BREATHE THE AIR
OF THE PLANET WE INHABIT.
WE ONLY KNOW HERE
HOW ALIVE WE ARE
KNOWING THAT WE WILL DIE
SOMETIMES, BUT NEVER
WE WILL KNOW WHEN.
SO THEREFORE KNOW
WE CAN ONLY SAY
MAY LUCK PROTECT US

THE UNIVERSE PROTECT US
AND FILL US WITH BLESSINGS
SO THAT WE DO
NOT LACK REFUGE,
COMFORT, PROTECTION,
WISDOM
TO MAKE THE DECISIONS
AND THAT WITH
HIS GREAT LOVE
MAY GOD
ALL POWERFUL
BECAUSE WE ARE
INNOCENT SINNERS
FOREVER AND EVER
SOMEDAY HE
WILL FORGIVE US.

*

"THE MOON AND I, WITH A STAR"

THE MOON AND I,
WITH A STAR
WE TALK ABOUT
BEAUTIFUL THINGS;
WE TELL EACH OTHER
SECRET CONFIDENCES
THEY ARE SO BEAUTIFUL
AND PRECIOUS
THAT ARE
ALWAYS PROTECTED
IN THE SILENT NIGHT.
THE MOON AND I
WITH A STAR
WE CROSS THE WHITE MIST;
THE MOON LIGHTENS
MY SLOW STEPS
AND I GIVE HER
MY FRANK SMILE.
SHE LAUGHS COLDLY ACTIVE
OF THE LONELY MOMENT.
THE MOON AND I,
WITH A STAR
WE ARE IDENTIFIED.
SHE LOVES ME VERY MUCH
AND I LOVE HER MORE.
THE MOON AND I,
WITH A STAR
WE FEEL ACCOMPANIED
SHE GIVES ME HER
RAY OF LIGHT
BECAUSE WE ARE

IN LOVE
WE KNOW FROM THE HEART
FROM FAR AWAY WE ARE
EMBRACED.

*

"HE"

HE WAS
THE HEIGHT OF CONTEMPT;
HE WAS LIKE A MESS.
I DON'T KNOW HOW
FAR THE RIDICULE REACHED,
OR IT WAS THE DEVIL'S MOCKER;
BUT MY LOVE WAS SO CLEAN
THAT BECAME DRAMATIC;
OF REALITY AND JEALOUSY,
OF SIN AND FORGIVENESS,
OF IMPOTENCE, OF PAIN
FOR THE TRAGIC IDYL
OF HIS INCOMPREHENSION.
ALL FOR HIS DETACH,
ALL FOR HIS HEARTFALL.
HE WAS A DUMPED SIGH;
HE WAS A
STRONG COMPULSION
A PITY, A GREAT SHAME
FOR MY HEART.
HE WAS A SAD TEAR
THAT REMAINED STATIC
WITHOUT REASON.
THAT TEARS OUR SOUL
WITHOUT ANY COMPASSION.
HE WAS A FAILURE, A MADNESS,
A GOODBYE OF TENSION;
IN A SIMPLE WORD
"THANK YOU"
FOR HIS LACK OF VALUE.
"HE WAS A FOX, UNGRATEFUL

AN INDOLENT WITH MY LOVE;
WHAT WAS SO INDIFFERENT
THAT I NEARLY DIED FOR,
BECAUSE HE DIDN'T CARE.
HIS FAREWELL WAS EVIL
BECAUSE HE DIDN'T SMILE AT ME
HE LEFT ALONE WITHOUT
LOOKING BACK;
WITHOUT EVEN SAYING
SO LONG!
IT WAS A FORGOTTEN
IN THE DISTANCE
A LOVE THAT DIED.

*

"DECLINE OF SHADOWS"

PASSION MAKES ME WALK
BEHIND A REMOTE ILLUSION;
WHICH FORM AN
INTERNAL CONFLICT
IN MY ROCK SOUL.
A SITUATION THAT
DOES NOT TRUST
WAITING FOR THE
CULMINATING CLIMAX
OF THE LONGED
ENCOUNTER.
ATTACKS THAT ARE
NEUTRALIZED,
BRAKES THAT DO NOT
LOOSE;
DESPERATE SECONDS
AND TRAITORY IMPATIENCE.
A PRUDENT DISTANCE,
TO LET YOU HEAR
THE BEAT OF MY HEART
WHO CRIES.
LONELINESS IT LOOKS LIKE
A DECLINE OF SHADOWS;
FOR NOT HAVING
A HIGH DEGREE
SITUATED LOVE
IN THE HEAT OF THINGS.

*

"TO DO OR NOT TO DO"

IF YOU DON'T DO IT TODAY
TOMORROW YOU CAN DO IT.
IF YOU DID IT YOU
WILL KNOW WHY.
IF YOU DO OR YOU DON'T,
THAT IS YOUR DECISION;
IF YOU LIVE IT OR
YOU DON'T LIVE IT
IT WILL BE YOUR RESOLUTION.
IF YOU DID IT OR YOU DIDN'T
WHAT YOU HAD TO DO
AT THE TIME
OF DETERMINATION
THERE WILL BE DOUBT
OR SATISFACTION.
IF YOU DO IT,
THE MARK WILL LEAVE
THAT YOU DID IT.
IF YOU DID NOT DO IT,
IT WILL REMAIN
THE TORTURE OF WHY?
IF YOU DON'T DO IT,
WHAT DID YOU LEAVE?
I STAY? OF THAT
WHICH WAS NOT DONE.
WHAT WAS NOT DONE
WHAT WAS INTENDED TO DO.
WHAT DID YOU LEAVE?
FOR LEAVING HIM WAITING
MAYBE ANOTHER TIME.
IT WAS NOT DONE, NO, NO;

THE MOMENT WAS
NOT ACHIEVED
AND TIME PASSED.
YOU LOST THE OPPORTUNITY,
IT WAS POSTPONED FOR
ANOTHER OCCASION;
THE DEAR DREAM WAS
NOT REALIZED,
THE COLD OF THE
SEPARATION LEFT.
THE NECESSARY MOMENT
HAS PASSED TO DO IT,
IT WAS VANISHED,
IT WAS GONE WITH THE WIND.
AND HE OR SHE DID IT
PERHAPS, WITH ANOTHER BEING;
IT IS NATURAL BECAUSE EVERY IDYL
ENDS IN THE ROMANTIC BED.
IT IS THE BEST WAY
TO LOVE YOURSELF;
WE ARE FROM
THE ANIMAL KINGDOM...
IT'S FOR THAT SIMPLE REASON
WHAT WE MAKE LOVE.
DOING IT IS THE TENDEREST JOY,
BY SURRENDERING
OUR BODY TO SEX.
BY MUTUAL AGREEMENT
ALWAYS,
OF COURSE.
FOR PURE LOVE,
FOR PURE TASTE;
BECAUSE EVERYTHING IS:
IF YOU LIKE IT,

OR IF YOU DON'T LIKE IT AT ALL.
THEY ARE STIMULUS,
COLORS
AND FLAVORS
TO DELIGHT US
OR REJECT THEM;
TO LAUGH OR TO CRY...
WITH ALL FEELINGS.
TO BE REBORN LATER
OF A BURNING KISS;
TO RETURN AGAIN
AFTER THE FAREWELL;
TO SUPPORT ALSO
ANY HARD RIGOR
ANY CRAZY TORMENT;
TO NEVER REMEMBER
THE ERRORS OF THE PAST
AND FORGET ALL THE AGONY
SUFFERED IN YESTERDAY.
TO REALIZE THAT
SUPREME DESIRE
LONG DESIRED.
TO LOVE EVEN MORE;
TO SHUT AN OPEN VOICE
IN THE DARK SILENCE;
TO LIVE THE FEARS
OF THE MYSTERY;
TO SING HYMNS
TO THE PASSION;
JOY IS NEEDED;
TO FEEL THE LOVE
WITHOUT HAVING
ANY NIGHTMARE;
TO FLY HIGH, EXALTED

DRESS OF
THE SACRED MANTLE
OF WONDERS.
AND BE ABLE TO MAKE
THE LEAP
HIGHER TO THE POOL.
TO BE ABLE TO EAT CALMLY,
AND BE HAPPY WITH MYSELF
DAY AFTER DAY.
SO THAT MORE POEMS
AND SONGS
SPROUT OF MY SOUL.
SO THAT WHEN I
WAKE UP AT DAWN
CONTINUE THE PARTY
OF MY LIFE.

*

"SHE IS"

HE IS NOT
A FRIEND GUY;
SHE IS A JUST A FRIEND;
THAT IS ALWAYS WITH ME
IN MY CRAZY WALK;
I'M WALKING HAPPY
ALONG WITH HER;
AND AT NIGHTS
SHE MAKES ME DREAM.
HAPPY, GLAD
WITH HER,
I SMILE, SOMETIMES,
OF HAPPINESS…
THINKING OF OTHER BEINGS
THAT THEY WOULD LIKE HER,
OR THAT THEY SEEK
HER WITH ANXIETY.
IF THEY KNEW THAT I HAVE IT
AND I SERVE IT WITH LOYALTY,
THEY WOULD ENVY
ME CONSTANTLY
AND THEY WOULD LOOK
FOR ANOTHER EQUAL.
TODAY I INTRODUCE HER TO YOU
BEAUTIFUL AND GOURGEOUS …
HERE I BRING HER WITH ME,
YOU CAN NOW LOOK AT
MY FRIEND IS NOTHING ELSE
THAT MY FAITHFUL COMPANION
THE SOLITUDE.

*

"FOR THE LOVE"

FOR THE LOVE!
FOR THE LOVE!
ALL TOTAL DELIVERY
OF FEELINGS
THAT LEAD TO HAPPINESS.
FOR LOVE, YOU NEED
BE SURE TO PROVIDE
SEXUAL PLEASURE...
WHAT THE LOVER
WISHES TO ACHIEVE.
IT IS NECESSARY FOR LOVE;
THE WAR OF THE SENSES,
THE SURPRISE OF
THE UNEXPECTED
THE RIGHT WORDS,
THE SILENT COMPLAINT
OF THE SOUL,
TO FULFILL THE
IMPRECIOUS MISSION
AS PROMISED.
IT IS NECESSARY FOR LOVE
THE PLACE FOR
THE REALIZATION
AND KEEP THE
SECRET WELL KEPT
AFTER OUR COMMUNION.
FOR LOVE YOU NEED
LOVING TOO STRONG
AND FIND SOMETHING NEW
IN EVERY INSTANT OF CARESSING,

TO MAKE IT LAST
THE PASSION OF LOVERS.
AND LOVE BE
UNFORGETTABLE.

*

"LOVED"

LOVED, KISSED, CARESSED
THIS IS HOW I FEEL TODAY,
WHEN I AM BY YOUR SIDE.
TOUCHED, TEMPT, SWEETENED,
I DON'T KNOW HOW YOU THINK,
BUT I FEEL SPELLED.
PRAISED, CALMED, DRUNKEN,
THIS IS HOW I WANT
TO FEEL TODAY
WHEN I HAVE HUGGED YOU.
STUCK, TIGHT, ALTERED,
I WANT TO STAY LIKE
THIS WITH YOU
WHEN WE'RE FINISHED.
FLATTERED, FASCINATED,
DELIGHTED
THIS IS WHAT I WANT
TO FEEL MY HONEY
WHEN YOU KISS ME
AND I HAVE KISSED YOU.
RAPTURED, SINLESS,
I DON'T KNOW IF THIS IS LOVE
BUT I AM LOVING NOW.
LOVED, ADOREDED, HAUNTED,
I DON'T KNOW WHAT YOU FEEL
BUT I FEEL PASSIONATE.
SITTING, LYING, STANDING
MAKING YOU HAPPY LOVE
FEELING WELL LOVED.

*

"WITH MYSELF"

AND YOU LEFT ME
WITH MYSELF
AND YOU LEFT ME
WITH MY LONELINESS;
WE SAID GOODBYE,
SEE YOU TOMORROW
TO BEGIN AGAIN.
AND YOU
LEFT ME WITH MYSELF;
AND YOU
LEFT ME WITH
MY REALITY.
THIS AFTERNOON
VERY IN LOVE
I HAD TALKED TO YOU
VERY EXCITED
OF ALL THE HAPPINESS
AND
OF EVERYTHING
WHAT IS OURS FOR
BOTH OF US;
I HAD TOLD YOU
THAT A GOOD FRIEND
IS THE MOST BEAUTIFUL
THING ABOUT LOVE;
YOU ACCOMPANIED ME
TO MY HOUSE,
BUT YOU DID NOT
ENTER FOR FEAR;
YOU SAID ME
GOODBYE KINDLY

AND YOU LEFT ME
AT THE PORTAL;
YOU JUST SMILED AT ME
YOU DIDN'T GET TO KISS ME;
AND YOU WENT AWAY,
QUIETLY,
WITHOUT LOOKING BACK,
TO LOOK AT ME, TO LOVE ME
TO MAKE STRONGER
OUR FRIENDSHIP.
TO KISS YOU, TO LOVE YOU
TO FEEL OUR TRUTH.
AND YOU LEFT ME
WITH MYSELF,
TO NOT FORGET YOU,
TO DREAM,
TO WAIT FOR YOU,
PATIENTLY,
TO WAIT FOR YOU
UNTIL THE END.
AND YOU LEFT ME
WITH MYSELF,
UNTIL TOMORROW,
FOR NOT FORGET
THAT YOU LEFT ME
WITH MYSELF,
THAT YOU LEFT ME
WITH MY ANXIETY.
AND YOU SAID
GOODBYE AS ALWAYS
SILENT, NOTHING MORE...
AND YOU WERE
WALKING SLOWLY
WITHOUT EVER THINKING...

THAT YOU LEFT ME
WITH MYSELF
SO NOT TO FORGET YOU,
TO DREAM,
TO WAIT FOR YOU PATIENTLY
TO SAY FAREWELL
AT THE THRESHOLD
AND YOU LEFT ME
WITH MYSELF
TO REMEMBER YOU,
TO CRY
AND YOU LEFT ME
WITH MYSELF
AND YOU LEFT ME
WITH MY LONELINESS.

*

"FROM THE GARDEN TO HEAVEN"

THE PETALS OF A ROSE
THEY BATHED MY
SOUL IN CARNATION;
YOU SAW ME IN THE LAUREL
WITH YOUR BUTTERFLY LIFE;
AND I FELT A THING,
LIKE A LILY OF THE VALLEY;
I FELT THERE ON THE STREET
A SAD AND CLOSE NOISE;
IT WAS YOUR HEART
THAT IN VAIN
IT SHINE LIKE A VIOLET;
AND FEELING LIKE
A WEATHERCOCK
I TURNED AROUND AND LEFT,
AND THE ALL ALLELIES DIED
OF YOUR PROMISES OF LOVE;
EQUAL TO THE
BEAUTIFUL FLOWER
FROM THE GARDEN OF EDEN.
YOU REMAINED LIKE A WHIPPET
ALONE, SAD AND FAR;
LIKE A PINK CHRYSANTHEMUM
FULL OF CACTUS AND IVIES;
LIKE A LAKE WITHOUT STONES,
CLEAN AS A MIRROR;
WITHOUT REVIVING DREAMS
OF THE THOUGHTS WE FORGET.
YOU LOOKED LIKE A CRACKED PINE
AND LIKE A BIRD OF PARADISE;
YOU LOOKED LIKE THE SPELL

OF THE AZHAR FULL OF THORNS,
YOU LEFT WITH YOUR
WOUNDED SOUL
FOR CUPID'S TEARS.
AND SO WITH MY
WOUNDED HEART
I WILL NOT THINK ABOUT
YOU ANYMORE;
AND SLEEPING IN
THE CRIMSON,
ON MY BED OF ORCHIDS,
I WILL BE DELIVERED
IN THE GRASS.
WITHOUT ANY NIGHTMARE.
LATER WHEN I WAKES UP;
YOU WILL NO LONGER BE...
I WILL LOOK VERY FAR THERE,
THERE ON THE HORIZON
AND I WILL SEE
A SUN AND A MOUNTAIN
WHITE AS FOAM;
I WILL SEE CAMELIAS!
I WILL SEE FEATHERS!
AND IT WILL NOT BE
THE IMAGINATION;
I WILL WALK AND
FIND A BRIGHTNESS
AND A LIGHT ON
MY PATH...
AND I WILL WALK
AMONG THE CLOUDS
BREATHING THE MIST;
AND I WILL SEE THE WONDERS!
WITHOUT FEELING ANY BADNESS.

AND EVERYTHING HAS TO BE MINE,
WITHOUT ANGUISH, OR REGRETS;
BECAUSE I WILL NOT SEE AGAIN
THE STREETS OF
MY IMMENSE GARDEN;
NOW I'LL BE ON A CUSHION,
SITTING THERE IN HEAVEN;
AND I WILL COVER MYSELF
WITH THE VEIL
OF BLESSED HAPPINESS;
AND I WILL TAKE A WAND,
FLASHING FLASHES.
AND I WILL NOT FEEL
JEALOUSY ANYMORE,
MAY MARTYRIZE MY HEART,
BECAUSE I HAVE
STOPPED BEING PASSION,
TO BE A LITTLE STAR;
THAT WILL SHINE ALONE,
THERE, THERE IN
THE WATCHTOWER;
AND I WILL BATHE
IN THE BEACH
OF ALL MY YOUTH,
TO HAVE A SET
OF NUANCES OF COLORS,
BECAUSE LOVE
WILL NOT EXIST
IN THIS PRECIOUS SKY.
I WILL DRINK WATER
FROM THE WELL
OF BLESSED HAPPINESS
I WILL PULL UP A MOTE
FROM A GOLDEN CLOUD;

AND I WILL SIT
ON THE THRONE
OF THE CHARIOT
OF THE IMMORTALS;
LOOKING INTO THE PORTALS
WITH THE COUPLES
OF THE EARTH,
AND TO THOSE WHO LIVE
IN THE CAPITAL,
SO THAT THEY DIE
WITHOUT MERCY
IN THE THRESHOLD
IN FRONT OF A CHURCH;
SO THEY DON'T
FORGET THE KISSES
NOT NOR
THE PRETTY LOOKS
AND SO THAT THEY
DON'T WASTE THE TIME
DEFOLIATING DAISIES.

*

Havana, June 26, 1977

"MAKING POETRY"

AND I WAS LEFT ALONE
AND SAD
IN THIS OLD HOUSE,
MAKING POETRY;
TO FORGET THAT
LOVE THAT LIVED HERE.
I WAS LEFT ALONE
WITHOUT YOU,
AND SO MUCH I LOVED YOU.
YOU CAUSED THE DISCONCERN
OF THE TIE THAT UNIT US.
NOW WHERE ARE YOU?
FEEDING YOURSELF
WITH GRIEF...
TO NEVER RETURN
TO THE HOME THAT
YOU HAD BY MY SIDE.
DON'T YOU WANT
TO COME BACK AGAIN?
TO BRIGHTEN THIS EMPTY HOUSE
AND FORGET ALL THE ERRORS
TO START LIVING DIFFERENTLY,
TO LOVE OURSELVES
WITH MORE PASSION;
TO FEEL, INTENSELY, LOVE
AND FILL US WITH JOY...
BUT YOU WENT AND LEFT ME
IN THIS OLD AND SAD HOUSE
MAKING POETRY
IN MY LONELINESS;
TO NOT GO OUT

TO LOOK FOR YOU
AND ASK YOU
TO COME BACK TO ME.
MAKING POETRY
I WILL CONTINUE
WAITING FOR YOU,
EVEN IF YOU
NEVER RETURN.

*

S.F. November 3, 1987

"NOT EVEN"

I DON'T EVEN THINK
ABOUT YOU;
I DON'T EVEN LIKE YOU...
EVEN IF I LET MYSELF BE DRIVEN
BY UNSURPASSED DIRECTIONS.
I ONLY FEEL HAPPY,
SOMETIMES WHEN
YOU LOOK FOR ME;
I DON'T WANT
TO DISAPPOINT YOU;
BUT IT'S NOT MY FAULT.
THAT I NOT FEEL ANYTHING
FOR YOU;
I THOUGHT IT COULD BE...
BUT THE IDEA WAS NULL.
I DON'T WANT
TO UNDERSTAND YOU...
AND I THINK I LIKE IT,
MAY YOU CARE A DREAM
AND YOU THINK
THAT I WANT YOU,
THAT YOU ARE MY PASSION...
AND MY MADNESS.
IT ANNOYS ME
WHEN I SEE YOU,
MAY YOU FEEL
SO MUCH TENDERNESS
WHEN I PASS BY YOUR SIDE
SINGING TO THE MOON
DON'T THINK
ABOUT ME ANYMORE;

CONTINUE YOUR HAPPY PATH;
AND LIFE ENJOY, BECAUSE
I DON'T EVEN
THINK ABOUT YOU
I DON'T EVEN LIKE YOU.

*

"JOINED"

WE ARE UNITED BY
AN INVICIBLE THREAD
WHICH LEADS US
TO DEATH.
WE ARE UNITED BY
DIVINE PROTECTION
EVERYONE WITH
THEIR GOOD
OR BAD LUCK.
WE ARE UNITED
TO THE EARTH THAT
FEEDS US.
WE ARE UNITED BY
THE AIR WE BREATHE.
WE ARE UNITED BY
BLOOD TIES
WHAT WE INHERIT.
WE ARE UNITED BECAUSE
WE ARE HUMAN
WE ARE UNITED BECAUSE
WE ARE BROTHERS.
WE ARE UNITED BY
A SACRED POWER.
WE ARE UNITED BY
THE SUN AND THE MOON
THROUGH THE STARRY SKY.
WE ARE UNITED BY
THE LOVE OF GOD
WE ARE UNITED BY
THE HATE OF THE DEVIL
WE ARE UNITED BY

THE MYSTERY OF LIFE
WE ARE UNITED BY
THE WATER WE DRINK.
WE ARE UNITED,
EVEN IF WE DID
NOT WANT TO BE TIED.
WE ARE UNITED
WITHOUT BEING
ABLE TO FREE OURSELVES.
WE ARE UNITED BY
THE MAGNETIC FORCE
OF THE PLANET WE INHABIT.
WE ARE UNITED ONLY
TO SAVE US.

*

"THE POWER"

POWER TO DO
EVERYTHING I WANT
POWER TO ACHIEVE
EVERYTHING I WANT.
POWER TO PERFORM
ALL MY BEAUTIFUL DREAMS.
I ONLY WANT POWER
AT THIS TIME
WHERE ALMOST
EVERYTHING IS MONEY.
CONTROL TOTAL POWER
FROM THE WHOLE UNIVERSE
THAT IS THE AMBITION OF SOME
HIGH HEADS OF GOVERNMENTS.
BEING ABLE TO LIVE WITHOUT
TROUBLESHOOTING
FEARS AND FEARS
IT IS THE ILLUSION OF MANY
WHO ARE BORN DISTRUSTING
UNDER THIS IMMENSE SKY.
POWER TO EXTERMINATE
FROM THE EARTH
THE RIDICULOUS JEALOUSY
OF THE MINDS
AND THE TERRIBLE WARS
WOULD BE
SOMETHING IDEAL FOR
FINISH IT ONCE
WITH THE IGNORANT AND
WITH THE DAMN MISERY.
POWER BUILDS
POWER DESTROYS

THE POWER OF LIFE
THE POWER OF DEATH
THE POWER OF THE RICH
THE POWER OF THE POOR
THE POWER OF THE NOBLES
THE POWER OF THE WICKED.
POWERFUL POWERS MAN HAS
WITHOUT BARELY KNOWING
HOW TO USE THEM.
THE POWER OF GOOD
AND THE POWER OF EVIL
THEY JOIN AT A TIME WITH
THE POWER OF THE SEA.
THE POWER OF THE UNIVERSE
IS VERY STRONG
CREATOR OF LIFE AND DEATH.
BEING ABLE TO SPEAK, BE ABLE
TO SCREAM AND SING
BE ABLE TO LAUGH
BE ABLE TO CRY AND BE SILENT.
BEING ABLE TO LIVE
IN ABSOLUTE FREEDOM
WITHOUT BEING ABLE
TO HIDE THE WHOLE TRUTH.
BEING ABLE TO SAY
WITH SINCERITY
WHAT THE POWER OF
FRIENDSHIP CAN.
SO MANY POWERFUL POWERS
THERE IS IN THIS ROUND WORLD
WHERE WE ALL CAN
HAVE SOME NATURAL POWER
TO ACHIEVE WHAT WE WANT
EVER PERFORM.

*

"NOTHING NOR NOBODY."

NOTHING AND NO ONE
CAN AVOID IT:
NOT NOR THE BURNING
HEAT OF THE GOBI DESERT
NOT EVEN THE FULL MOON OF
THE GLACIAL NIGHTS
NOT NOR THE HELL FIRE
OF SATAN
NOT NOR THE VALLEY OF
A THOUSAND HILLS
NOT WHETHER HEIGHTS
NEITHER THE DARK SEA IN WINTER
NOR RICHARD HEART OF LION.
NEITHER THE KING OF GOLD,
NOR THE KING OF CUPS
NEITHER THE QUEEH OF STICK,
NOR THE ACE OF SWORDS
ANY WITH
RED OR BLACK HEARTS
NOT CINDERELLA'S
CRUEL STEPMOTHER
NOT ALICE IN WONDERLAND
NOT EVEN THE GENIUS
OF ALADINN'S LAMP
NOT NOR
THE QUEEN OF THE FAIRIES
NOT EVEN THE UGLY
WITCHES OF SALEM
NOT SNOW WHITE AND
THE SEVEN DWARFS
NOT CAT IN BOOTS

NOT EVEN THE WOLF OF
THE LITTLE RED RIDING HOOD
NOR MANDRAKE THE WIZARD
NOT COUNT DRACULA
NOT FRANKENSTEIN
NOT EVEN THE VAMPIRE
OF DUSSELDORF
NOT EVEN THE MONSTER
OF THE BLACK LAGOON,
NOT EVEN
THE PYRAMIDS OF EGYPT
NOT EVEN WONDER WOMAN
NOT EITHER THE HOUND
OF THE BASKERVILLES
NEITHER SUPERMAN,
NOR BATMAN
NOT EVEN SPIDER-MAN
NOT NOR THE STORM CAPTAIN
NOT EVEN THE RAINS OF RANCHIPUR
NOT NOR THE ACTIVE VOLCANOES
OF THE EARTH
NOR THE TREASURES
OF KING SOLOMON
NOT NOR THE MASK OF THE ZORRO,
NOT NOR THE VALIENT PRINCE
NOT ALÍ BABA AND THE 40 THIEVES
NOT EVEN THE MONA LISA
NOT NOR THE ICHI MASSEUSE
NOT EVEN THE HEROINE MULAN
NOT NOR THE BLIND OICHI
NOT THE FOG OF LONDON
NOT NOR THE REVENGE
OF THE WEREWOLF
NOR THE EVIL

ENVY OF THE WICKED
NOT NOR
THE EXTERMINATING ANGEL
NOR BEINGS FROM OTHER PLANETS
NOT EVEN THE FLYING SAUCERS
NOT NOR THE VIRGIN WAX
FROM THE HIVES
NOT NOR THE SANDS OF
THE SAHARA DESERT
NOT NOR THE BLACK BIRDS OF EVIL
NOT EVEN THE LONE RANGER
NOT NOR THE WITCH CIRCE
NOT EVEN THE SNOW
OF KILIMANJARO
NOT NOR THE GOZZILA BEAST
NOT EVEN THE KILLER BEES
NOT EVEN THE PIRANHAS
OF THE AMAZON RIVER
NOT NOR THE RED FISHES
NOT MOBYDICK THE WHITE WHALE
NOT THE THREE MUSKETEERS
NOT NOR THE COUNT
OF MONTECRISTO
NOT THE BAD MESSALINA
NOT NOR THE SWAMP OF THE SOULS
NOT NOR THE DISCIPLES OF THE DEVIL
NOT NOR THE PHANTOM OF THE OPERA
NOT THE REBELLION OF THE GLADIATORS
NOT NOR THE FOUR HORSEMAN
OF THE APOCALYPSE
NOT NOR THE ABOMINABLE SNOWMAN
NI JIM FROM THE AFRICAN JUNGLE
NOR TARZAN THE APE MAN
NOT THE COLOSSUS OF RHODES

NI FU MAN CHU, NI CHAN LI PO
NOT ANY CHINESE DOCTOR
NOT POISONOUS SNAKES
NOT NOR THE BOMBAY STRANGLERS
NOT EVEN THE THREE WISE MONKEYS
NOT THE AZTEC MUMMY
NOT EVEN THE SNOW QUEEN
NOT NOR THE GIRL WITH
THE MATCHES
NEITHER POLYPHEMUS,
NOR ULYSSES
NOT NOR THE IRON MAN
NOT NOR THE BLACK SCORPION
NOT EVEN THE GREATER ANACONDA
NOT THE BLACK MAMBA
NOT NOR THE HUNCHBACK OF
NOTRE DAME
NOT EITHER THE CRIMSON PIRATE
NOT EVEN THE SEVEN SAMURAIS
NOT DOGS WITH RABIES
NOT EVEN THE BENGAL TIGERS
NOT NOR THE LION OF THE METRO
NOT NOR THE NIGHT BUTTERFLIES
NOT EVEN THE COLD OF
THE NORTH POLE
NEITHER THE STORMS,
NOR THE SUNAMIS
NOT NOR THE EARTH QUAKES
NEITHER TYPHUS, NOR
WHOOPING COUGH
NEITHER CHICKENPOX,
NOR EBOLA
NEITHER POLIO,
NOR YELLOW FEVER

NOT NOR THE DEADLY AIDS
NOT NOR MALARIA
NEITHER TETANUS,
NOR SMALLPOX
NOT TUBERCULOSIS
NOT EVEN THAT FATAL
CORONA VIRUS
NOTHING AND
NO ONE EVER
YOU WILL NEVER
BE ABLE TO ACHIEVE
END THE BLESSED
HUMAN GENEROSITY.

*

"FLOWERS OF FLESH"

WE ARE FLOWERS OF FLESH
IN THE ORCHARD OF LIFE
WITHERING US
UNDER THE BLUE SKY
BLACK OR RED
OF TIME PASSING
RELENTLESS
WITHOUT FEELING
EVERY SECOND
THAT DOES NOT FORGIVE
LIKE THE DEEP SEA
AND VORAZOUS.
WE LIVE IN THIS FERTILE
PLANET CALLED EARTH
WHERE WE ARE
BORN INNOCENT
EXCLUSIVE CREATURES
OF CAST LUCK
BY DESTINY...
LET US HAVE TO LIVE.
IT WILL EACH ONE'S TURN
YOUR MISSION AT BIRTH
IN YOUR BEAUTIFUL COUNTRY
WHERE ONIPOTENT GOD
FROM ETRNITY
OF THE FIRMATION
KNOW WHAT WILL HAPPEN
WITH US
THE EARTHLY MORTALS
THAT WE LIVE WAITING
FOR SOMETHING

UNDER THIS GREAT SUN
THAT WILL BURN OUR WINGS
HOW FLOWERS BURN
AND THE VARIED ROSES
THAT EMBELLISH
AND PERFUME
THE BEAUTIFUL GARDENS
FROM THIS
MYSTERIOUS WORLD
AND THEY DIE WITHER
WHEN THE NIGHT FALL.

*

"THE BEAUTY"

THE BEAUTIFUL THING IN LIFE
IS THE JOY OF LIVING
EVERY DAY AND ENJOY
THE WARM NIGHTS
AND COLD WITH
THE SAME HAPPY LOVE.
BEAUTIFUL IMPRESSES US
AND DELIGHTS THE LOOK.
THE MAGNIFICENCE
OF THE FINE ARTS,
IT MAKES US FEEL THAT
ONLY EMOTION
OF HAPPINESS.
WE ARE LOVERS
OF GENUINE BEAUTY,
OF PERFECTNESS.
WHAT IS BEAUTIFUL CAN BE
VERY CONTRADICTORY,
WHAT IS BEAUTIFUL CAN
DISTURB SOME MINDS.
BEAUTY CAN BE
DISCOVERED SUDDENLY
BEAUTY IS ALWAYS
KNOWN TO APPRECIATE
FROM DIFFERENT
POINTS OF VIEWS.
FOR THE BEAUTIFUL
HUMANS LIVE,
FOR THE BEAUTIFUL
WE LOVE AND VALUE.
THE GREENEST

BEAUTY THERE IS
IT EXISTS INSIDE
NOT ON THE OUTSIDE.
THE PHYSICAL THING
IS CONSIDERED BEAUTIFUL
FACE, ARMS, HANDS, LEGS
BEAUTIFUL HAIR,
EYEBROWS, BEARDS.
UNIQUE LANDSCAPES
THAT IT OFFERS US
THE WISE NATURE.
EVERYTHING SOMEHOW
IT CAN BE BEAUTIFUL TO US.
EVERYTHING IS BEAUTY.

*

"DEATH DOES NOT EXIST"

DEATH ONLY EXISTS
WHEN
YOU FORGET ABOUT
THE DECEASED.
BECAUSE IN OUR WORLD
NO ONE COMPLETELY
DISAPPEARS.
AS LONG AS
WE DON'T FORGET
THOSE THAT PASSED AWAY.
THEY WERE FAITHFULL
WHO ARE GONE FROM US,
THOSE MAGNIFICENT BEINGS
WE LOVE SO MUCH IN LIFE.
THEY WILL BE WITH US
IN OUR HEARTS ALWAYS.
AT ANY TIME WE REMEMBER
THEM WITH LOVE
THEY WILL BE REBORN
IN OUR THOUGHTS
REMEMBERING THEM,
RELIVING
THOSE PAST DAYS
THAT WE ENJOY TOGETHER.
I AM VERY SURE TO KNOW
THAT:
TRUE DEATH IS WHEN
YOU COMPLETELY
FORGET EVERYTHING.
EXPERIENCES ALWAYS LAST
IN THE MIND AND

IN THE HEART.
THE ONLY TWO SITES
WE HAVE
TO SAVE THOSE FANCY
IN DELETABLE MEMORIES
OF OUR BELOVED EXISTENCE.
DEATH CAN ONLY
EXIST ON THIS EARTH
WHEN WE MANAGE
TO FORGET THOSE WE LOVE
AND ONE DAY
WITHOUT WANTING,
THEY DEPARTED
INTO ETERNITY!

*

"THE IMMENSITY"

WE LOOK INTO THE FAR
AND SEE
THE IMMENSITY!
THE ONE OF THE OPEN SKIES
THE ONE FROM THE FAR LAND
THAT OF LONG AND SHORT TIME
THE MYSTERY OF NOTHING
THAT OF DAILY LIFE
THAT OF EXPECTED DEATH
THE ONE OF THE SAVED MEMORY
THAT OF INFINITE PENALTY
THAT OF HIDDEN SUFFERING
THE ONE OF THE QUIET ANGUISH
THE ONE OF A HAPPY HEART
THAT OF THE SUCCESS ACHIEVED
THE ONE OF DAMNED REVENGE
THAT OF PROVOKED ANGER
THE ONE WITH THE SIMPLE SMILE
THAT OF ETERNAL BITTERNESS
THAT OF FELT PRIDE
THAT OF THE JOY OF LIVING
THAT OF BREATHE DEEP
THAT OF KNOWING HOW
TO LAUGH AND CRY
THAT OF EXPECTED
FORGIVENESS
THE ONE OF THE LAST HOPE
THAT OF THOSE FIGHTERS
THAT OF PAST CENTURIES
THAT OF THE IGNORANT ALL
THAT OF THE POOR INNOCENTS

THE ONE OF THE KNOW-IT-ALLS
THAT OF THE TERMINALLY ILL
THE ONE OF THOSE
WHO SOW HATE
THE ONE OF THOSE
WHO NEVER ARRIVED
THE ONE OF THOSE
WHO WERE DYING
THE ONE OF THOSE WHO
UNWANTINGLY STAYED
THAT OF THE SOLDIERS OF WAR
THAT OF HONEST CIVILIANS
THAT OF EXPECTED FORGIVENESS
THAT OF THE SIN COMMITTED
THE ONE OF THOSE WHO
EXPECT SOMETHING
THE ONE OF THE FULL MOON
THE SUN IN SUMMER
THAT OF BEING
AMONG DARKNESS
THE ONE OF EVIL DOUBT
THAT OF THE SURVIVORS
THE EXTENSION OF ALL THINGS
WILL ALWAYS EXIST IN US
LET'S LOOK TO THE HORIZON
TO THE INFINITE IMMENSITY.

*

"YEAR OF THE TIGER"

Don't be scared, no.
Don't even tell yourself to run
Because we are now
In the Year of the Tiger
but I'm not going to scratch you
with my feline claws
I'm not even going to bite you
With my sharp fangs.
Although you know
that I am a beast
When the desire provokes me
Of fighting with challengers
Which are dangerous
and also
Silent doing harm
To present humanity
I will be ready when
That long-awaited
moment has arrived
From the aforementioned
meeting destined
'Physically and mentally
I will challenge you'
To beat you and continue
Being the winning tiger
In this magical city
SAN FRANCISCO!

*

February, 22, 1986

"SKINS"

SKINS OF BEINGS OF THE EARTH
SKINS CLASSIFIED BY THEIR COLOR
THIS IS THUS THE HUMAN RACE
WAS BORN
FULL OF PRIDE AND SPLENDOR.
THE SKIN PROTECTS US
FROM COLD AND HEAT
AND DISTINGUISHES US BY
IDENTIFYING US
IN THIS WORLD OF LOVE.
THAT DIVIDES AND CLASSIFIES US
ACCORDING TO THE DEGREE
OF PIPMETATION.
FROM THE
CREATE CIVILIZATION.
THEY CALL THOSE
WITH DARK SKIN BLACKS
NATIVES OF
THE AFRICAN CONTINENT
BURNED BY THE STRONG SUN
ASIANS ARE YELLOW SKINNED.
THE INDIANS ARE RED
OR BROWN SKINS.
THE SKIN PROVIDES
SEXUAL ATTRACTION
TO ANOTHER DIFFERENT
SKIN THAT FEELS
THE STRONG PASSION.
THE SKIN CAUSES LOVE AND HATE
WE LIVE TO SAVE THE SKIN
ALTHOUGH BE ANY COLOR.

*

"INSPIRATION"

TO ACHIEVE A RESPONSIVE
LOVE POEM
YOU HAVE TO BE VERY IN LOVE.
THEN THE DIVINE MIRACLE EMERGES
THE INSPIRATION OF THE SOUL
THAT IS BORN ALONE,
SPONTANEOUS
AND ALLOWS YOU
TO TELL THE LOVED ONE
THE HEARTFUL SINCERE WORDS
THAT YOU WILL LISTEN
WITH PLEASURE
COMING TO MOVE YOUR SOUL.
FULL OF HAPPINESS ACHIEVED.
WE ARE BOTH BLESSED TODAY
I LOVE AND LOVE ME INTENSELY
KISS AND KISS WITH ALL
MY PASSION.
I FEEL VERY HAPPY TODAY
WITH WHAT I HAVE.
WE FEEL FULLY
MADE TODAY.
HOW LONG OUR IDYLL LASTS
IT WILL BE WHAT GOD WANTS.
BUT NOW I CAN SAY
THAT I HAVE ACHIEVED
THIS TRIUMPH
SO GREAT OF LOVE.

*

"WHAT WE DESERVE"

YOU DESERVE WHAT
YOU BELONG TO HAVE
EVEN THOUGH YOU ALWAYS
WANT SOMETHING BETTER.
WHAT YOU EXPECT AND
DID NOT EXPECT TO RECEIVE
OF THE LIFE YOU HAD TO LIVE.
WE ARE DESERVING
TO HAVE GOOD HEALTH,
MONEY AND FINDING LOVE.
TO REALIZE YOUR DESIRES
AND PLANS,
TO HAVE GOOD COMPENSATION.
FIGHT FOR WHAT IS WORTH IT
IT IS TO ACHIEVE
THE GREATEST SATISFACTION.
FIGHTING FOR A JUST CAUSE IS
DESERVE A RECOGNIZE
OF HONOR.
AND FOR THOSE EVIL CRIMINALS
THAT CAUSE DESTRUCTION,
IT WILL COME TO
YOU SOONER OR EARLY
RECEIVE YOUR
DESERVED PUNISHMENT
AND THEY WILL
HAVE NO SALVATION.
DESERVING WE ARE
THOSE WHO STILL ALIVE
TO ENJOY ALL
BEAUTIFUL THINGS,

HEALTHY AND DELICIOUS
THAT LIFE GIVES US.
WE DESERVE TO LIVE
IN PEACE AND HARMONY
IN THIS WORLD WHERE
WE WERE BORN
TO DESERVE DIVINE GRACE
AND THE GRACE OF GOD.

*

"IT IS NOT MINE"

THIS IS NOT MINE, BUT I REPEAT IT,
SOMEONE FROM THE PAST SAID IT
AND IT IS GOOD THAT
YOU DON'T FORGET TODAY:
"The colors have been made to taste, and
for the gardens the varied flowera too."
WE LEARN WISELY IF WE READ
THE SAYINGS THAT
EXIST OF HUMANITY
WHICH PREVAIL
FOR ALL ETERNITY.
IN THIS WORLD EVERYTHING
HAS A REMEDY
MINUS THE INEVITABLE DEATH
MAY IT REACH US ALL SOMETIME.
DEATH IS THE SUREEST
THING THAT EXISTS
NO ONE WILL BE SAVED
FROM DIE IN THIS WORLD.
CURRENTLY THERE
ARE ONLY VALID
SOME FOOTPRINTS OF THE PAST
LIKE LATENT EVIDENCE
OF EVERYTHING THAT HAPPENED
SINCE THE BEGINNING
OF THE PLANET
ALTHOUGH
TO CERTAIN SCIENCE
NO ONE ENSURES
WHAT REALLY HAPPENED.

*

"LIMITATIONS"

I THINK EVERYTHING
HAS ITS LIMIT
EVEN IF SOME SAY NO.
BECAUSE ONE WHO
GOES OVER HIS LIMIT
WILL PERISH' DUE
TO ITS MISTAKE,
AND DON'T WILL
SENSE ANY ALTERATION
UNTIL WHEN WE
SHOULD STAND
A HEAVY BURDEN
OR A HUMILIATION.
HOW MUCH IS
THE LIMIT OF SUFFERING?
WHAT IS THE LIMIT OF PAIN?
UNTIL YOU CAN LIVE...
IN POVERTY OR DESPERATION?
WE MUST LIMIT OURSELVES
TO ACCEPTING WELL
WHAT WE CAN DO
AND WHAT WE CAN'T.
WE LIVE FULL OF LIMITATIONS
THAT CONTROLS US
ALL THE PASSION.
OUR STOCK IS LIMITED
TO ACHIEVE SALVATION.
LIMITING OURSELVES
WE ALL LIVE
TO ACHIEVE OR

NOT TO ACHIEVE
OUR EFFECTIVE SOLUTION.
LIMITED WE ALL ARE
EVEN IF SOME SAY NO.

*

"THE OTHERS AND ME"

THE OTHERS PERHAPS...
THEY ARE DEAD
AND ONLY ME WITH LOVE
I'M HERE TO TELL
WITH VALOR
THINGS THAT THEY
NEVER THOUGHT.
THE LIVE OF OUR SOULS...
THEY NEED ASK FOR
OUR COMMUNICATION;
THE FEAR WILL BE
AWAKE EARLY
AND ANOTHER DAY...
I WILL LIVING WITHOUT
ANY WORD FROM YOU;
ANOTHER DAWN
OF LONELINESS
IT WILL BE FAREWELL
IN SILENCE,
AND I WILL KNOW
NOTHING
WHAT I WILL TO SAY
ABOUT WHAT HAPPANED
BETWEEN US.
THE OTHERS SOULS
PERHAPS...
THEY DON'T
UNDERSTAND ENOUGH WELL
WHAT I WILL FEEL WHEN
I CAN TALK TO YOU;
I THINK THAT WE WILL BE

LAUGH A LOT, ALSO,
WE WILL GOING
TO FEEL SOMETHING NEW
THAT NOBODY FELT BEFORE;
THE OTHERS PERHAPS...
THEY ARE DEAD
AND I HERE ONLY
CONSOLING YOU...
TO TELL WITH
ABSOLUTELY SERENITY
THAT, WHAT ONLY
IN PRIVATE
CAN COMMUNICATE
TO YOU
WITH LOVE!

*

"SUFFER"

I SUFFER AND I
CONTINUE SUFFERING
FOR THE DIFFERENT SUFFERINGS
OF OUR HUMAN RACE.
SUFFER FOR IT
IT MAKES ME FEEL MORE RELIEF
WHEN FEELING THAT INTENSE PAIN
OF THOSE PEOPLE WHO IN DIFFERENT
COUNTRIES SUFFER GREAT PENALTY
FOR A MISFORTUNE T
HAT HAS OCCURRED.
PURE CRY OF THE SUFFERING SOUL
BITTER TEARS OF THE HEART.
JOIN THEM ALL FOR SUFFERING
WE SUFFER AND CRY TOGETHER
BECAUSE OF WHAT
HAS HAPPENED TO US
IN OUR LIFE.
SUFFERING THE DEEP STRUGGLE
FOR SURVIVING IN THE PLACE
WHERE WE HAD TO BE BORN;
TO FULFILL OUR DESTINY.
ACCORDING TO WHERE
WE ARE BORN
WE CAN SUFFER LESS,
BUT WE WILL
ALL SUFFER A LOT
FOR SOME REASON
THOUSANDS OF
DIFFICULT REASONS
WHAT HUMANS HAVE

TO SUFFER AND
SUFFER FOR THAT
REASON.
WARS HAVE MADE SUFFER
TO ALL GENERATIONS
ACCORDING TO
THE HOLY SCRIPTURES;
WE ALL SUFFER AND EVEN
THE RICH SUFFER A LOT
AND THEY CRY FOR A PENALTY.
WE ARE VERY STRONG OF SPIRIT;
WE ARE CREATED ON THIS PLANET
TO SUFFER AND TO LOVE.
I SUFFER AND I WILL SUFFER TOO
FOR THOSE WHO SUFFERED A LOT
IN PAST CENTURIES, ESPECIALLY
OF THE SUFFERINGS
OF THE 20TH CENTURY.
THE FIRST AND
SECOND WORLD WAR.
THE HORRORS THEY SUFFERED
THOSE INNOCENT JEWS
IN THOSE MACABRE
CONCENTRATION CAMPS.
WAR CRIMES,
MISTREATMENT
OF CHILDREN AND WOMEN.
THE IMMENSE SUFFERING
OF THE ILLEGALS WHO CROSS
THE FRONTIER TO ACHIEVE
A BETTER FUTURE IN LIFE.
ENDURING YEARS SUFFERING
JUST FOR USA ARRIVE,
TO LIVE AND DIE.

WHAT WILL BE?
WHAT WILL BE?
NOT ONE KNOW
BUT WHILE
WE ARE LIVING
WE WILL KNOW!

*

www.ingramcontent.com/pod-product-compliance
Lightning Source LLC
Chambersburg PA
CBHW070753120626
46557CB00002B/582